LONGMAN IMPRINT BOOKS
Autobiographies

Selected and edited by
Linda Marsh

Cover photograph by
Catherine Shakespeare Lane

D1638453

LONGMAN

Longman Imprint Books
General Editor: Michael Marland CBE MA

*Cassette available

Contents

Introduction

autobiography: a person's life, written by herself or
himself

auto, self   *bio*, life   *graphein*, to write

'We are our memories,' wrote Edna O'Brien, but, 'The
memories that lie within us are not carved in stone,'
wrote Primo Levi.

Here is one difficulty in writing an autobiography;
time distances us from the things we did, the thoughts
we had, the people we met. So how can we be sure that
we're remembering correctly?

William Cooper sums it up for people who have a
long life to look back on:

> 'I've always said I can't write an autobiography, for
> the simple reason that I can't remember what
> happened. When I was young my memory was below
> par; now I'm old it's beyond hope.'

But he says that on the first page of his autobiography,
From Early Life, so he can't have been too put off! How
did he go on to fill another 168 pages? And what makes
people write the story of their lives?

This is what Laurie Lee wrote:

> 'A day unremembered is like a soul unborn, worse
> than if it had never been. What indeed was that

summer if it is not recalled? That journey? That act of love? To whom did it happen if it has left you with nothing? Certainly not to you. So any bits of warm life preserved by the pen are trophies snatched from the dark, are branches of leaves fished out of the flood . . . '

Primo Levi, surfacing from the dark and terrible waters of his time as a Jew in Auschwitz, wrote *If This Is a Man* 'to bear witness'. 'I cannot tolerate the fact that a man should be judged not for what he is but because of the group to which he happens to belong.'

Almost all autobiographies have in common that sense of the excitement, the joy, the sorrow, the poignancy and the urgency of recapturing the writer's life in words, and creating new understandings of all the things that happened. This is true of young writers with just a few years, a few significant moments to reflect on, as well as older writers surveying a whole lifetime.

The autobiographical extracts in this book are all written by British writers or writers who have made their homes in Britain, and they look with feeling at 'the Seven Ages of Man', at life in the country and in cities, at life at home and on the road, in peacetime and in war. It is *their* lives that they evoke and explore, but they also speak to us about our own, for the very best autobiographical writing is both uniquely personal and yet also able to touch on the similarities of human experience that transcend circumstances, place and time. The journey of self-discovery takes us on wider roads than we might suppose; '. . . after we have examined ourselves,' wrote Ngugi Wa Thiongo, 'we radiate onwards and discover peoples and worlds around us.'

Linda Marsh

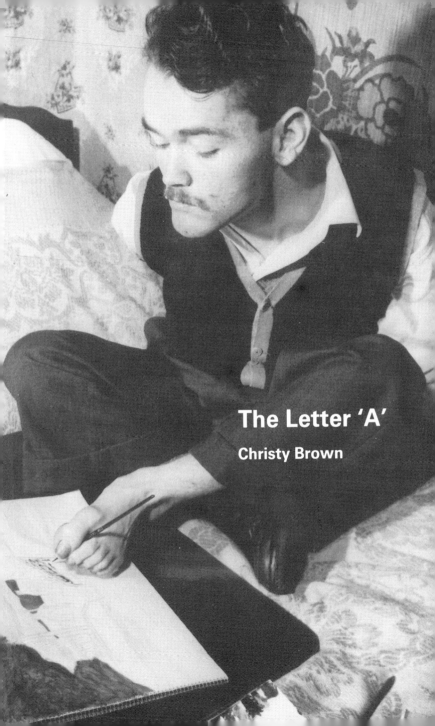

The Letter 'A'

Christy Brown

Christy Brown

The Letter 'A'

From *My Left Foot*

Christy Brown was born with cerebral palsy, and he could not control his speech or his movement. Almost every doctor said he was a 'hopeless case'; they said that he was mentally defective and nothing could ever be done for him – so why not put him away in an institution?

> *'Never!' said my mother almost fiercely, when this was suggested to her. 'I know my boy is not an idiot. It is his body that is shattered, not his mind. I'm sure of that.'*
>
> *Sure? Yet inwardly, she prayed God would give her some proof of her faith. She knew it was one thing to believe but quite another to prove.*

I was born in the Rotunda Hospital, on June 5th, 1932. There were nine children before me and twelve after me, so I myself belong to the middle group. Out of this total of twenty-two, seventeen lived, four died in infancy, leaving thirteen still to hold the family fort.

Mine was a difficult birth, I am told. Both mother and son almost died. A whole army of relations queued up outside the hospital until the small hours of the morning, waiting for news and praying furiously that it would be good.

After my birth mother was sent to recuperate for some weeks and I was kept in the hospital while she was away. I remained there for some time, without name, for I wasn't baptised until my mother was well enough to bring me to church.

It was mother who first saw that there was something wrong with me. I was about four months old at the time. She noticed that my head had a habit of falling backwards whenever she tried to feed me. She attempted to correct this by placing her hand on the back of my neck to keep it steady. But when she took it away back it would drop again. That was the first warning sign. Then she became aware of other defects as I got older. She saw that my hands were clenched nearly all of the time and were inclined to twine behind my back; my mouth couldn't grasp the teat of the bottle because even at that early age my jaws would either lock together tightly, so that it was impossible for her to open them, or they would suddenly become limp and fall loose, dragging my whole mouth to one side. At six months I could not sit up without having a mountain of pillows around me; at twelve months it was the same.

Very worried by this, mother told my father her fears, and they decided to seek medical advice without any further delay. I was a little over a year old when they began to take me to hospitals and clinics, convinced that there was something definitely wrong with me, something which they could not understand or name, but which was very real and disturbing.

Almost every doctor who saw and examined me, labelled me a very interesting but also a hopeless case. Many told mother very gently that I was mentally defective and would remain so. That was a hard blow to a young mother who had already reared five healthy children. The doctors were so very sure of themselves that mother's faith in me seemed almost an impertinence. They assured her that nothing could be done for me.

She refused to accept this truth, the inevitable truth – as it then seemed – that I was beyond cure, beyond saving, even beyond hope. She could not and would not believe that I was an imbecile, as the doctors told her. She had nothing in the world to go by, not a scrap of evidence to support her conviction that, though my body was crippled, my mind was not. In spite of all the doctors and specialists told her, she would not agree. I don't believe she knew why – she just knew without feeling the smallest shade of doubt.

Finding that the doctors could not help in any way beyond telling her not to place her trust in me, or, in other words, to forget I was a human creature, rather to regard me as just something to be fed and washed and then put away again, mother decided there and then to take matters into her own hands. I was *her* child, and therefore part of the family. No matter how dull and incapable I might grow up to be, she was determined to treat me on the same plane as the others, and not as the 'queer one' in the back room who was never spoken of when there were visitors present.

That was a momentous decision as far as my future life was concerned. It meant that I would always have my mother on my side to help me fight all the battles that were to come, and to inspire me with new strength when I was almost beaten. But it wasn't easy for her because now the relatives and friends had decided otherwise. They contended that I should be taken kindly, sympathetically, but not seriously. That would be a mistake. 'For your own sake,' they told her, 'don't look to this boy as you would to the others; it would only break your heart in the end.' Luckily for me, mother and father held out against the lot of them. But mother wasn't content just to say that I was not an idiot, she set out to prove it, not because of any rigid sense of duty, but out of love. That is why she was so successful.

At this time she had the five other children to look after besides the 'difficult one', though as yet it was not by any means a full house. There were my brothers, Jim, Tony and Paddy, and my two sisters, Lily and Mona, all of them very young, just a year or so between each of them, so that they were almost exactly like steps of stairs.

Four years rolled by and I was now five, and still as helpless as a newly-born baby. While my father was out at bricklaying earning our bread and butter for us, mother was slowly, patiently pulling down the wall, brick by brick, that seemed to thrust itself between me and the other children, slowly, patiently penetrating beyond the thick curtain that hung over my mind, separating it from theirs. It was hard, heart-breaking work, for often all she got from me in return was a vague smile and perhaps a faint gurgle. I could not speak or even mumble, nor could I sit up without support on my own, let alone take steps. But I wasn't inert or motionless. I seemed indeed to be convulsed with movement, wild, stiff, snake-like movement that never left me, except in sleep. My fingers twisted and twitched continually, my arms twined backwards and would often shoot out suddenly this way and that, and my head lolled and sagged sideways. I was a queer, crooked little fellow.

Mother tells me how one day she had been sitting with me for hours in an upstairs room, showing me pictures out of a great big storybook that I had got from Santa Claus last Christmas and telling me the names of the different animals and flowers that were in them, trying without success to get me to repeat them. This had gone on for hours while she talked and laughed with me. Then at the end of it she leaned over me and said gently into my ear:

'Did you like it, Chris? Did you like the bears and the monkeys and all the lovely flowers? Nod your head for yes, like a good boy.'

But I could make no sign that I had understood her. Her face was bent over mine, hopefully. Suddenly, involuntarily, my queer hand reached up and grasped one of the dark curls that fell in a thick cluster about her neck. Gently she loosened the clenched fingers, though some dark strands were still clutched between them.

Then she turned away from my curious stare and left the room, crying. The door closed behind her. It all seemed hopeless. It looked as though there was some justification for my relatives' contention that I was an idiot and beyond help.

They now spoke of an institution.

'Never!' said my mother almost fiercely, when this was suggested to her. 'I know my boy is not an idiot. It is his body that is shattered, not his mind. I'm sure of that.'

Sure? Yet inwardly, she prayed God would give her some proof of her faith. She knew it was one thing to believe but quite another thing to prove.

I was now five, and still I showed no real sign of intelligence. I showed no apparent interest in things except with my toes – more especially those of my left foot. Although my natural habits were clean I could not aid myself, but in this respect my father took care of me. I used to lie on my back all the time in the kitchen or, on bright warm days, out in the garden, a little bundle of crooked muscles and twisted nerves, surrounded by a family that loved me and hoped for me and that made me part of their own warmth and humanity. I was lonely, imprisoned in a world of my own, unable to communicate with others, cut off, separated from them as though a glass wall stood between my existence and theirs, thrusting me beyond the sphere of their lives and activities. I longed to run about and play with the rest, but I was unable to break loose from my bondage.

Then, suddenly, it happened! In a moment everything was changed, my future life moulded into a definite shape, my mother's faith in me rewarded and her secret fear changed into open triumph.

It happened so quickly, so simply after all the years of waiting and uncertainty that I can see and feel the whole scene as if it had happened last week. It was the afternoon of a cold, grey December day. The streets outside glistened with snow; the white sparkling flakes stuck and melted on the window-panes and hung on the boughs of the trees like molten silver. The wind howled dismally, whipping up little whirling columns of snow that rose and fell at every fresh gust. And over all, the dull, murky sky stretched like a dark canopy, a vast infinity of greyness.

Inside, all the family were gathered round the big kitchen fire that lit up the little room with a warm glow and made giant shadows dance on the walls and ceiling.

In a corner Mona and Paddy were sitting huddled together, a few torn school primers before them. They were writing down little sums on to an old chipped slate, using a bright piece of yellow chalk. I was close to them, propped up by a few pillows against the wall, watching.

It was the chalk that attracted me so much. It was a long, slender stick of vivid yellow. I had never seen anything like it before, and it showed up so well against the black surface of the slate that I was fascinated by it as much as if it had been a stick of gold.

Suddenly I wanted desperately to do what my sister was doing. Then – without thinking or knowing exactly what I was doing, I reached out and took the stick of chalk out of my sister's hand – *with my left foot.*

I do not know why I used my left foot to do this. It is a puzzle to many people as well as to myself, for, although I had displayed a curious interest in my toes at an early age, I had never attempted before this to use either of my feet in any way. They could have been as useless to me as were my hands. That day, however, my left foot, apparently on its own volition, reached out and very impolitely took the chalk out of my sister's hand.

I held it tightly between my toes, and, acting on an impulse, made a wild sort of scribble with it on the slate. Next moment I stopped, a bit dazed, surprised, looking down at the stick of yellow chalk stuck between my toes, not knowing what to do with it next, hardly knowing how it got there. Then I looked up and became aware that everyone had stopped talking and were staring at me silently. Nobody stirred. Mona, her black curls framing her chubby little face, stared at me with great big eyes and open mouth. Across the open hearth, his face lit by flames, sat my father, leaning forward, hands outspread on his knees, his shoulders tense. I felt the sweat break out on my forehead.

My mother came in from the pantry with a steaming pot in her hand. She stopped midway between the table and the fire, feeling the tension flowing through the room. She followed their stare and saw me, in the corner. Her eyes looked from my face down to my foot, with the chalk gripped between my toes. She put down the pot.

Then she crossed over to me and knelt down beside me, as she had done so many times before.

'I'll show you what to do with it, Chris,' she said,

very slowly and in a queer, jerky way, her face flushed as if with some inner excitement.

Taking another piece of chalk from Mona, she hesitated, then very deliberately drew, on the floor in front of me, *the single letter 'A'*.

'Copy that,' she said, looking steadily at me. 'Copy it, Christy.'

I couldn't.

I looked about me, looked around at the faces that were turned towards me, tense, excited faces that were at that moment frozen, immobile, eager, waiting for a miracle in their midst.

The stillness was profound. The room was full of flame and shadow that danced before my eyes and lulled my taut nerves into a sort of waking sleep. I could hear the sound of the water-tap dripping in the pantry, the loud ticking of the clock on the mantelshelf, and the soft hiss and crackle of the logs on the open hearth.

I tried again. I put out my foot and made a wild jerking stab with the chalk which produced a very crooked line and nothing more. Mother held the slate steady for me.

'Try again, Chris,' she whispered in my ear. 'Again.'

I did. I stiffened my body and put my left foot out again, for the third time. I drew one side of the letter. I drew half the other side. Then the stick of chalk broke and I was left with a stump. I wanted to fling it away and give up. Then I felt my mother's hand on my shoulder. I tried once more. Out went my foot. I shook, I sweated and strained every muscle. My hands were so tightly clenched that my fingernails bit into the flesh. I set my teeth so hard that I nearly pierced my lower lip. Everything in the room swam till the faces around me were mere patches of white. But – I drew it – *the letter 'A'*. There it was on the floor before me. Shaky, with awkward, wobbly sides and a very uneven centre line. But it *was* the letter 'A'. I looked up. I saw my mother's face for a moment, tears on her cheeks. Then my father stooped down and hoisted me on to his shoulder.

I had done it! It had started – the thing that was to give my mind its chance of expressing itself. True, I couldn't speak with my lips, but now I would speak through something more lasting than spoken words – written words.

That one letter, scrawled on the floor with a broken bit of yellow chalk gripped between my toes, was my road to a new world, my key to mental freedom. It was to provide a source of relaxation to the tense, taut thing that was me which panted for expression behind a twisted mouth.

Buchi Emecheta

How They Told Me

From *Head Above Water*

Buchi Emecheta comes from Nigeria, and Head Above Water *is the story of her struggle to bring up her five children alone after coming to live in England. She was determined to be a writer, and her dream came true when her first book,* In the Ditch, *was published in 1972.*

Here is the powerful recollection of her birth, as told to her by 'Big Mother', her father's elder sister, at home in Ibusa.

Most of the events that happened before I was born had to be told to me by my mothers. The history of the British Empire and her greatness I learned from my English teachers at school in Lagos. But when it came to events that happened nearer home, concerning my ancestors and me in particular, I had to rely on the different versions told to me by my mothers. They never ceased to fascinate me, especially as each member of my family had a slightly different version. It was from this oral source that I learned from many angles the story of my birth.

My father, right from the time I could first remember, had always called me Nnem – 'my mother'. And my mother had always referred to my moodiness and the mysterious habit I had of refusing food in order to attract attention as coming 'not from my side of the family but from that mysterious woman who gave her father birth'. I grew up under the shadow of this. But it was my big mother, my father's elder sister, Nwakwaluzo

Ogbueyin – this woman whom I see constantly when I look at my image in the mirror; this soft, very fat woman who seemed to have all the patience in the world; this mysterious woman who had the art of punctuating her stories with long silences and deep breathing – it was she who had the patience to tell it all to me in one go.

It happened the third day after our arrival in Ibusa. We had finished eating our evening meal and I could hear my cousin Ogugua shouting:

> *'Umu nnunu, umu nnu nta*
> *Tunzanza tulu nza*
> *Unu no nebo eme gide*
> *Tunzanza tulu nza . . .'*

I always loved this moonlight call: 'Little birds, little birds, come out in front of Ededemushe's compound and dance with little bells in front and cowrie shells at your back . . .'

By the time she reached the end of her call-song, many of us were puffing at the feet of Nwakwaluzo Ogbueyin. We gasped our final response of '*Tinzanza tulu nza*' as we collapsed onto one another in a big heap, and wrestled ourselves playfully free on the white brilliant sand at Otinkpu.

My big mother, whom we called Nneayin Ogbueyin (Our Mother the Elephant Killer), laughed in her slow rich voice and cautioned, 'Little children, my little children, you have just eaten your evening meal, you don't want to regurgitate it do you?'

'No, we don't!'

'Then sit down and sing your *inu* song once more.'

We obediently sang '*Umu nnunu umu nnu nta*' once more and the *inu* song of 'Agadi Nwayin' (The Old Woman who Lost her Sons) and by the time we did the last chorus of 'Zomilizo' the echoes of our young voices went from one sand clearing and one part of Ibusa to another. At that moment it seemed to me as if every compound had emptied its young ones onto the moonlit sand to celebrate the joy of living and the joy of the new moon.

As our voices died, an indescribable peacefulness spread over us. We looked up to this magnificent woman with silver hair that fitted her like a cap, at her back, glistening and full face, and tried to peer into those brown eyes – eyes which we knew were becoming weaker and weaker as she progressed towards her grave. We studied her stick, lying between her legs like a rod of life as she sat there on her stool, and we looked up at her with expectancy to tell us what else to do.

'Do you want to sing once more?' We could hear the rich rumble of amusement in her belly.

'No, mother, we want stories!'

'I can't hear you.'

'We want stories, we want stories, stories, tell us the story of Agadi Nwayin, please tell us our own Ogbueyin!'

She had succeeded in rousing our curiosity and expectancy and she knew it. She closed her eyes and slowly drifted into one of her story-telling trances. And when she opened her mouth to speak, the voice that came out was distant and mesmerising.

'Whose father walked seven lands and swam seven seas to fight and kill a bad man called Hitilah?'

'It's me,' I whispered hoarsely, afraid of disturbing the quiet grip her voice was having on us.

'Who is our come-back mother Agbogo?'

'It's me.' This time I could not restrain myself any longer. I stood up proudly and this movement of mine startled all my little relatives sitting there on the sand at

Otinkpu into reality. 'It's her, it's her,' their voices chorused. 'It's me, it's me,' I screamed intermittently.

'Who has a mother that can write and read like white people?'

By this time, I was dancing around singing '*O nmu. O mu.*' (It's me, it's me.)

Our excitement reached a deafening pitch, which amused her not a little. It was obvious that that night's *inu* story was going to be about me. And years later I could see why I was particularly singled out for this treat – the treat of being the heroine of our big mother's *inu* story.

Her real name, Nwakwaluzo, means 'this child cleared the path'. She was apparently expected to clear the path for some male children. She was only a girl child, so a man child was expected after her. It was almost like a command: she must have a male baby brother. I used to wonder sometimes what would have happened if, having given her such a name, her mother had had another baby girl instead of my father. Nonetheless, my father did come after her, although much, much later, and was given the name Nwabudike – 'this child is a warrior'. Although my big mother was a woman, through her strength and achievement she acquired the title Ogbueyin – 'the killer of elephants'. Words had it that she had led some elephant hunts, because she used to deal with the sale of their tusks. But by the time we were born she was getting old and looked more like a grandmother than a big aunt, and due to the ignorant activities of many like her, elephants had long disappeared from that part of West Africa. However, she kept the relics of her great days. She had huge anklets and bracelets made from the tusks of grown elephants. Most people were supposed to wear such huge and cumbersome ornaments only on special occasions. Not

Big Mother! She had hers chiselled in such a curious fashion that she bathed with them on, she slept with them on, and she walked with them, a feat that required not only a unique skill but a lot of energy too.

When my brother Adolphus and myself first saw this swaggering lady, we ran. We were terrified for we had never seen such a person in Lagos, where we were born. And when our big mother tried to embrace us, we let out such a scream that people did not stop talking about it for a long time.

As I stood afar, shaking from fear, I saw my big mother cry and my heart melted and I felt sorry for her. I saw her walk with bowed head into her hut. Curiosity got the better of me and I followed gingerly behind her and stood there by her little door as she took her pestle *odo* handle and cracked to pieces those expensive tusk ornaments. Presently, she came out with her arms open to us in welcome. Although my brother still ran away from her after this, I did not run too far. Encouraged by my hesitancy, she dipped her now naked hands into her *nbunukwu* – waist skirt – and brought out a dark shiny *eshi* fish that had been dried in the sun until it was dark and mouth-watering, and lured me to her with it. Then I ran to her and our relatives laughed. The knots of bystanders were horrified at the loss of her expensive tusk ornaments, but with my hand firmly clasped in hers she reminded them, with her face beaming, 'When has it ever been a virtue to be rich in wealth and poor in people?' The relatives nodded. They understood her very well – why have heaven and earth when you have no one to share it with?

With my free hand in hers and the other clutching the *eshi* fish, I looked up to the face of Big Mother. Never before had I seen anyone so full of happiness. And as a further treat she was that evening going to tell us the story of my birth. It was going to be my story, the story which she was going to cross seven lands and swim seven seas to get, just for me, because I was important. Because I was a significant person in our community at Umuezeokolo Odanta in Ibusa.

In her low, anaesthetising voice she began. 'Why all said "Ah, only a girl" to Alice Ogbanje Ojebeta and her husband Jeremy Nwabudike Emecheta when a little girl was born to them was understandable. What trouble did she not cause as she ran out of her mother's belly in seven months when other children stayed nine? And there was nothing like a premature baby unit at the Massey Street Dispensary in Lagos where she was born. Most normal mothers did not have to go to such places. But because this little girl came into the world before her time, her poor mother had to be taken to those white people's birth places. Her mother did not know what to do and neither did the people who helped her deliver the girl child. Many of them nodded knowingly, thinking that she would not live anyway. She was a little bigger than the biggest rat you've ever seen, all head. So those people from the hospital sent Alice Ogbanje home with her scrap of humanity. She could not take her to her husband because she felt shame. Because, you see, Nwabudike married his wife here, according to our custom, and then when they got to Lagos, he had to marry her again according to the laws of the white people. Ogbanje wore a long white dress with another white piece that looked like a spider's web on her head. This latter piece was long, and she had her friends to hold it for her so that she did not trip over it. They both looked funny, but who understands the ways of those strange white people? After they had been inside that house, a big one where they prayed to their god, everybody came and took photos, and all ate rice and meat and drank plenty of palm wine and then they all danced all night. It cost my brother Nwabudike a lot of money, I can tell you. All that nonsense.

'And then if a man had done all that for you, what type of child would you give him?'

'A bouncing baby boy howling with life on a banana leaf,' we replied, hypnotised.

'Well, Ogbanje did not do that. She presented Nwabudike with this scrap of humanity. So when she left that dispensary, she was crying, and the sky was crying with her, because the girl child arrived in July, our wettest month. She took her to her brother's wife.

"And what is this? I want to be sick," said her sister-in-law, Obi's wife.

"It's a child, a girl child," pleaded Ogbanje.

"She cannot live anyway," said Obi's wife. She should know because she had six children of her own, all boys and no girl.

'So they tucked the little wet bundle of flesh away with many rags to keep her warm, and dropped water into her bird-like mouth. But the girl child did not die. Instead she started to raise hell. Hm, what a voice she had. And her heart beat gbim, gbim, gbim.

'It was then that my brother Nwabudike saw in the child's determination to live the fighting spirit of our mother, Agbogo. And he too was determined to make his daughter live. But the daughter started to turn yellow. And Alice Ogbanje, because of the white training she had had in Onitsha, took her girl child and ran back to the hospital where she was born. She cried and said, "Look, my baby is turning yellow even though I gave her drops of water as my experienced sister-in-law advised. I know she has not got much chance of livng but my husband said that she is his come-back mother.

And he will not forgive me if I let his come–back mother die."

'And the nurses in Lagos, they took the law into their own hands. They hailed abuse onto Alice Ogbanje and they said to her, "How would you feel if someone fed you only drops of water for three days, eh? How would you feel?" One big Yoruba nurse threatened to beat her up, but took pity when she saw that Alice Ogbanje was still bleeding from the birth and that she was in-experienced.

'And those nurses stuck her virgin nipples into the child's mouth and she sucked and she sucked, and guess what!'

'She lived,' we all shouted.

And I got carried away and I added my ending to the story. 'And after a year, I brought a man child to the world, and my father and mother named him Adolphus Chisingali Emecheta!'

We clapped and danced that night. And I knew that I was forgiven for being born premature with a big head and small body and for being a girl, because I must have recommended my parents highly to the children living beneath the earth for Olisa to send my mother my brother, who arrived with no fuss, who stayed the whole nine months in her belly, and who appeared roaring his way into the world. And they did not need to tuck him up with rags.

My father and his friends must have been so proud of this strong, big baby boy that they named him after the man they thought was the toughest on earth – Adolphus Hitler. Sometimes as a child I used to wonder why my brother was called after the man whose very name we were later taught to fear. But then who knows what goes on inside the minds of ambitious, proud Ibo fathers? As most Ibo boys born around that time were called Adolphus after the German leader, Adol is still a fairly common name among the Ibos of Nigeria.

Whereas my brother was given the military names of Adolphus Chisingali Emecheta, meaning 'God has ordered my promotion', my mother decided to call me Florence in reminiscence of the story of the lady with the lamp which the missionaries had told her when she was in Onitsha. My father decided on Onyebuchi, meaning 'Are you my god?' The pet name Nnenna, meaning 'father's mother', was not recorded as he and he only could call me that, just as my brother was locally known as Hitilah.

How we heap titles and ambitions on our children! Even today in the mid-1980s I have never seen prouder parents than typical Ibo ones. We expect our children to conquer the world, we push them into conquering the world and when they fail to do so we find it difficult to forgive them. I know many Ibo men in Europe and America who will never go home because they have failed to live up to the names given to them by their parents and Umunna.

Beryl Bainbridge

Funny Noises with Our Mouths

From Granta: *Autobiography*

Beryl Bainbridge remembers her relations at home in Liverpool in the 1930's.

There weren't many places we could go. We lived in a house that should have been large enough for four, but my mother was preserving the rooms for visitors. The lounge and the dining-room were out of bounds and we occupied only two bedrooms out of the four available. It was generally understood that the mattresses in the other rooms were mildewed with the damp and unfit to lie on. My brother slept with my father and I kept my mother warm. I wouldn't have been surprised if I had caught my mother spraying the mattresses in the spare rooms with the watering-can – she'd have gone to any lengths to avoid sleeping with my father. If my brother got up in the night to go to the lav my father would shout, 'Turn that blasted light off. You're burning electricity.' That was when he was in a sour mood. If he was in a good mood he would call out jovially, 'Many there, son?' and laugh so much that he couldn't go back to sleep. Then he would pad downstairs in his overcoat and make himself a bacon sandwich.

The only room we were allowed to use – it was wisely never referred to as the living-room – was entirely filled with a table and chairs. I had to crawl under the table to get to my chair. My father sat jammed beneath the window-ledge, hunched over because the wireless jutted out. We ate our food as though any moment the Last Trumpet might sound. To this day I have never seen the point of lingering over a meal.

When we were older, my brother and I went out because we had grown too large to stay in. He went to the church, the bowling green and the youth club. I went to the pine woods and the sea. I liked it best when the wind blew strongly. All the time I was walking on the shore I kept looking for interesting objects. There were whole crates of rotten fruit, melons and oranges and grapefruits, swollen up and bursting with salt water; lumps of meat wrapped in stained cotton cloth through which the maggots tunnelled if the weather was warm, and stranded jellyfish, obscene and mindless. Several times I found bad things – half a horse and two small dogs. The dogs were bloated, garlanded in seaweed, snouts encrusted with salt.

When we were out, my mother usually sat upstairs reading a library book; if my father was on the rampage she took herself off to the railway station and read by the fire in the porters' room, pretending she was waiting for a train. My father listened to the wireless or paced the garden in the dark. Years later in a theatre, watching *Death of a Salesman*, I recognised the set, the light in the upstairs window, and Willie Loman – a dead ringer for my father – stumbling about the yard in a dream, muttering of business deals.

The only visitors that ever came to our house were my aunts, Margo and Nellie, and my maternal grandparents, Mr and Mrs Baines. At the height of the blitz, to be out of danger, my grandparents came to stay; but left after two days. My grandfather said he preferred to take his chances with the Luftwaffe. Of my aunts, Nellie was deferred to more than Margo, though Margo was the wage-earner. My mother didn't care for either of them, on the principle that they were related to my father.

Auntie Nellie had a touch of the martyr: she went to church and did the shopping. Whenever my father came in through the front door she made him lie down on the sofa. She said men were frailer than women. Auntie Margo was a dressmaker. She had been apprenticed when she was twelve to a woman who lived next door to Emmanuel Church School: hand-sewing, basting, cutting cloth, learning her trade. When she was thirteen they had given her a silver thimble. She sat at her sewing-machine as though she were playing the organ at the Winter Gardens in Blackpool, pulling out all the stops, head bowed, swaying on her chair, knee jerking up and down as she worked the treadle. When she broke off the thread she turned round, as if she heard applause behind her. For a time during the war she took a job in the munitions factory at Speke, but Auntie Nellie made her give it up. She said Margo was growing coarse. My mother said there were indications of hysteria in her appearance, a kind of giddiness. She wore cocktail dresses and white wedge-heeled shoes. She smoked continuously and her eyes were over-emphatic; they glittered with drama and fatigue. She bought a lot of the material for the dressmaking from shops that had been bombed, and seeing her in a frock of slightly charred cloth, a diamanté clasp at the hip and a scorch mark on the shoulder, she looked like a woman ravaged by fire. She made a fool of herself over a schoolmaster called Seymour, and there was the occasion, never to be forgotten, when the Dutch seaman billeted on them in the first year of the war had given her a length of satin from the East. Secretly, behind

Nellie's back, she'd sewn it up into a sarong – she wore it at a meeting of the Women's Guild, a slit up the leg and her suspenders showing beneath the baggy edge of her green silk drawers.

I stayed the night with my aunties once a fortnight. When they got ready for bed they put their flannel nightgowns on over their clothes and then undressed, poking the fire to make a blaze before they removed their corsets. They grunted and twisted on the hearthrug, struggling to undo the numerous hooks that confined them, until panting and triumphant, they tore free the great pink garments and dropped them to the floor, where they lay like cricket pads, still holding the shape of their owners, the little dangling suspenders sparkling in the firelight. Dull then after such exertion, mesmerised by the heat of the fire, the two women stood rubbing their nightdresses to and fro across their stomachs, breathing slow and deep. After a while they sat down on either side of the fender and removed their stockings. Out on to the woollen rug, at last, came their strange yellow feet, toes curled inwards against the warmth.

Mr Baines, my mother's father, was tall and portly. He was a director of Goodlass Walls, the Liverpool paint firm. He'd bettered himself with a vengeance and collected butterfly specimens. Before the war my grandfather had gone on cruises, leaving my grandmother behind; she had failed to rise with him. She was small and bent, and stored a humbug in her cheek. She made a habit of coming over queer whenever she went down town and accepting brandy from sympathetic passersby. My mother treated her with contempt and was always telling her to pull herself together. Her dislike of Grandma had to do with a dog called Bill. My mother had been given Bill as a little girl, on the understanding that it wouldn't make a mess of the garden. My grandma didn't like dogs, and she went out and dug all the daffodils and blamed it on Bill. My grandfather got rid of the animal the next day, though it broke his heart. My father said my mother was talking through her hat – 'The old bugger jumped at the chance,' he said. 'He was too mean to pay for its blasted food.' My grandma confided to me that she'd had rickets as an infant and that at ten she'd worked in a boiled-sweet factory in Gateacre. My mother said it was a dirty lie. If we went out to tea in Southport and my mother left a tip under the plate, my grandmother used to pick it up and slide it into her handbag.

Liverpool people have always been articulate, and my family used words as though they were talking to save their lives. Realities might be hidden, like income and insurance and sex, but emotions and judgements flowed from them like blood. If you sat in a corner being seen and not heard, in the space of a few moments you could hear a whole character being assassinated, dissected and chucked in the bin, to be plucked out and redeemed in one small sentence. Thus my mother, in a discussion with Margo concerning Auntie Nellie, would say how lacking in depth Nellie was, too dour, too big for her boots. And Auntie Margo, heaping on coals of fire, would mention incidents of malice and deceitfulness, my mother nodding her head all the while in agreement, until just as Nellie lay unravelled before my eyes, Auntie Margo would say, 'By heck, but you can't fault her sponge cake.'

There were always words in the house, even when we weren't speaking to each other. There was the wireless, balanced on the ledge behind the curtains. The valves never burned out, but it was cracked across the front in three places and had been patched with black adhesive. My mother wanted the wireless thrown out. Once, she nearly succeeded. She was upstairs at the time, shaking the bath-mat out of the window. It was damp and heavy and slipped from her fingers on to the aerial stretched from the outside wall to the top of the fence. The wireless bounced off the ledge and toppled between the chair and table. My father flung himself forward and caught it in his arms. He loved the wireless, not for music but for the voices talking about poetry and politics, which were the same thing for him.

Continually I try to write it down, this sense of family life. For it seems to me that the funny noises we make with our mouths, or the squiggles that we put on paper, are only for ourselves to hear, to prove there's someone there.

Clifford Dyment

My Father, the Carpenter

From *The Railway Game*

When Clifford Dyment was a boy, his family went to live in Nottingham in the house of the unpleasant Mrs Belton, their landlady. Mr Belton often sloped off to a secret room, filled with model railways . . .

A railway isn't just carriages and a locomotive and a permanent way. It's a sort of door. At any time you can open it and take to the road, turning your back on a home that's dreary and on a life that's a misery to you. Any time you fancy you can whizz off to a new home and a new life, in any place you choose. Whenever you're down in the dumps – just open the door.

Albert Belton

This experience helped Clifford Dyment to find wonder, enthusiasm and happiness at a difficult time in his young life.

Just before life with the Beltons, we meet Clifford's father:

My father liked to work with the woods of fruit trees, apple, pear, cherry, and he was fond of experimenting with timbers that are not much used, such as young sweet chestnut, laburnum, and holly. When he wasn't constructing some large piece of furniture he filled in his time fashioning small articles out of fragments that had taken his fancy: he made walking-sticks from buckthorn, snuff-boxes from maple, axe and hammer shafts from ash, egg-cups, napkin-rings, spoons, bowls, dolls, horses, little tables and chairs from beech, lime horse-chestnut, and elder. He was always on the look-out for a bit of promising timber somewhere under the sky. Our downstairs and upstairs were scented with sawn-up trees.

Tools were a familiar sight also. Near the window, covered with sacking during the day, was a lathe worked by a treadle; and in a corner there was a rough table used as a bench, fitted with a vice and a sawing-board. A spirit-level was sometimes left on the mantelpiece, a mallet on a chair. I didn't think there was anything odd about having wood and wood-working implements in your house: they were among the first things I fixed my gaze on and I accepted them as natural phenomena like fire and food and furniture. I took it for granted that everybody lived in a cottage like ours and had tools and timber in their living-room.

For my father, the purpose of life was doing rather than being; for him, therefore, to be idle was to be unhappy. His fingers had eyes at their tips, ceaselessly searching the world for jobs to be done. One of his favourite jobs – when he wasn't turning or mortising – was repairing old petrol lighters. I think he felt that he had a mission to perform among the maimed, the halt, and the blind lighters of Monmouthshire, seeing his duty plain to make the broken casing whole, the dull spark wheel bright, the crooked snuffer straight. He could never resist the appeal of a disabled lighter, and in consequence collected a whole infirmary of brass invalids from his friends and workmates. On these he would operate in our beautiful lamplight, patiently dismantling, cleaning, filing, oiling, polishing, rewicking, reflinting, rewadding, reassembling. Out of five sick lighters he would make three healthy ones, and these he would sell for shillings to the friends from whom he had bought them for pence.

But although – as the above shows – my father had a business sense as pushful as a bradawl he would never do a job for the money only. He enjoyed his tools and timber too much for that. It was only when he had given to some piece of work in wood all the time, experience, and care that were necessary and added a little more of each out of sheer affection – it was only then – that he became what he was commonly called, a tradesman, and began to think of costs and profits. And although he took only a small return for himself his prices had to be high, for he refused to deliver to a customer anything but perfection. He had many temptations. Because his products were home-made people expected them to be cheaper than the shiny, swollen, knobbly factory splendours they saw in the big shop windows of Newport Mon and Cardiff and were puzzled to find they weren't. My father explained. Sometimes the inquirers were willing to pay his price; more often they weren't. He never quoted a figure lower than the one he had originally given. Occasionally there were people who, after listening to the reasons for his high charges, said to my father: Couldn't you, just for this once, use not *quite* such prime timber, and couldn't you, just for this once, put not *quite* so much labour into it, couldn't you . . .? But my father always refused. He had only one standard.

All the same, I don't think my father was an artist. He was a good plain cook rather than a chef. His care was that all his materials should be wholesome and all his uses of them honest. For this reason he took just as much trouble over backs, which nobody sees, as with fronts; for this reason he would never use plywood to fill in large surfaces, but stuck to solid wood everywhere;

for this reason he preferred wax finishing to French polishing because it revealed the quality of the timber; and for this reason he hated veneers because they were deceptions and avoided carving, inlay, painting, gilding, graining, and moulding because he believed that virtue is intrinsic and not a matter of outward appearances. His aim was to maintain the tradition of the local craftsman, the man near the village green or on the market square whom you once went to when you wanted a new pair of boots, a carriage, a stool, an iron gate, or even a picture. He had no pretentious notions about this, however, and would have gone red to hear the phrase 'His aim was to maintain the tradition of . . .' used about him. He was no goody-goody, no Plymouth Brother of carpentry. He was worldly. He was ambitious. He wanted to get rich. But the object of getting rich for its own sake bored him. He thought of wealth not as gain but as reward – reward for work well done.

Naturally, my father's conception of work was costly in time as well as in materials and labour, so that nearly always in my memory of him he is handling wood and tools. I see him with the rosy satinness of planed boards of mahogany, with white holly and lime, fawn maple, close-grained hard box, mackerel-patterned pale oak, red cherry and pear and brown apple; I see loved and lovely implements taken out of their box one by one and laid on the floor in order to search for a dropped silver bit at the bottom; I see his plane skinning the plank and the plank swallowing his drill; and I see the hand-saw with its oily smile and its wolf's teeth eager to devour and I feel safer when my father puts on its leather muzzle.

My father's thoroughness wasn't confined to his work bench. All that he ever did was equally thorough. One

day when he was courting my mother he called un-
expectedly at her home in Bank Street, Newport Mon,
in order to take her out. He discovered that she'd
already gone out – with her father, into the country. My
mother's father was a great walker and a great man for
the countryside: my father was neither. Nevertheless, he
set out after them: he'd decided to be with my mother
that day and be with her he would. He followed the
elderly man and the young woman with unfaltering
tenacity, tracing their route by inquiries at cottages and
public houses and by noting places where my grandfather had plucked wild herbs and flowers. In the late
evening my mother and grandfather arrived home;
there, hours afterwards, my father caught them up: he
had taken exactly the same walk as they had, but had
taken it many miles in their rear.

Later, when they were a young married couple, he
and my mother were walking in the neighbourhood of
Caerleon; as they passed an oak tree growing near a
brook my father commented that it was a tree that
would cut up into nice timber. My mother forgot the
remark, but it wasn't an idle one on my father's part.
He'd taken a liking to the tree and had decided to have
it, for he was turning over in his mind the idea of
making a special adjustable armchair for the fireside
of 1, Ashwell Terrace. The more he thought about
it and the oftener he went to look at it the more
he was convinced that oak was just the timber he
wanted.

One black night, working by the glow-worm light of a
screened bicycle lamp, he cut the tree down and levered
it over the grass into the stream, where it sank into mud
and weeds and was hidden. On later nights, with the
help of two G.W.R. workmates with whom he had
arranged to share it, he sawed the oak trunk into planks

and again hid the wood in the stream. The railway line ran through the fields not far away, and on successive evenings my father and his friends transported the planks to the track, loaded them on to a wagon, attached the wagon to a goods train, and, at a point within walking distance of Ashwell Terrace, flung them overboard, afterwards jumping off the moving train themselves.

My father got his share of the wood home singlehanded, crossing several reens – Monmouthshire for ditches – by laying one of the planks across as a bridge and carrying the rest over on his shoulder. When he got the planks to the cottage he stacked them inside, telling my mother that he'd got them through a deal, because if she had known what he'd been up to she would have been scared stiff. Next day – he was so keen – he began work on the chair.

The exploit shows the lengths to which my father was prepared to go in order to get what he wanted. He stole the tree, yes; but I would defend him by saying that his was a *crime passionnel*, similar to that of the hard-up scholar who steals a desired book from a library or shop. Reprehensible it may be, but an act of love rather than of larceny.

Yes, as I've said, my father was no Plymouth Brother. In his teens, wanting to see the world but having no money to pay for travel, he signed on at Newport Mon as a ship's carpenter, giving a fluent and convincing account of his experience in that line. In truth, he'd never set foot on board a ship in his life, and when, in the Bay of Biscay, he heard squall-wet sailors calling out 'Chips! Chips!' he had no idea that the shouts were for him and remained in his bunk, sea-sick. Eventually, with a one-way voyage to his credit and therefore able to claim extensive knowledge of international ships and shipping, he joined another ship at Buenos Aires and worked his passage half around the world before returning to England and resuming his trade terrestrially. A man of ruses my father was, but they were never mean ruses: he had that romantic touch of the rascal so helpful to success in this world.

One day I saw my father walking about the cottage in stiff unaccustomed clothes.

'Your daddy is a soldier now,' Grandmother said.

But weeks before this we had all – Father, Mother, Susie, and I – gone on a train ride to Cardiff. It was a holiday, but I realise now that Susie and I enjoyed the excitement and the sunshine more than our parents, because the purpose of the Cardiff visit was to be photographed as a family group before we were broken up by my father's departure for France. He had volunteered for the army under Lord Derby's scheme and was expecting his call-up papers every day.

We took it in turns, Susie and I, to be hoisted on Father's shoulder and carried along the white, packed pavements and across the wide, racing streets. I'd never heard so many people, motors, carts, horses; never seen trams hiss by on flashing rails and wires, monster fireworks with men and women sitting comfortably inside. It was thrilling; and if it hadn't been for Father and Mother, frightening.

'This is the shop,' said Father, and we entered a large hushed gloom. After the pavements, treading the carpet was like walking on cushions.

'This way, please.'

A man with a head as bare as a lemon led us to the far end of the long room, and there by a miracle I was able to stand under a blue sky and look at trees, waves, and a boat. The man raised his arms and the fresh air was wafted to the roof. Where the sky and the trees and the waves and the boat had been there was now a broad marble staircase and pillars and ferny plants. The wizard looked at the marble staircase and then at us and – hey presto! – the marble staircase and the pillars and the ferny plants vanished and there was the blue sky again.

'You just there, sir; and your good lady, I think, just here; and you little ones, up you go!' and he lifted Susie on to a table. And then me. The man switched on lamps, full moons, and I couldn't see anything – not the man, not Susie, not Mother or Father: I looked into a fiery hurting nothingness. I cried.

After the readjustment of the lights I was given a walking-stick to hold. I saw a wooden box creep towards us; it stopped creeping and from behind it a golliwog popped up suddenly. I cried again. But the golliwog got rid of his darkness and became the man with a head as bare as a lemon. He gave me a pear drop to suck.

We all stood and sat quite still, my father soaring above us, pale and grave with the ends of his moustache given a special Sunday-best waxing and a curl upwards, my mother wearing her polite public expression, Susie believing in the dicky bird and I doubting.

Susie's faith was justified: a dicky bird did appear, a yellow fluffy chick with a red paper beak. The lemon man gave it to her for being so good.

There came the morning when my father put his feet one by one on a stool and bandaged his legs with puttees. Then on went the webbed belt, the leather bandolier, the flat peaked cap. He caught me up in his arms and hugged me and my face was hurt by one of his new buttons. He put me down and took up Susie. He kissed Grandmother, Mother. Then we all went to the door.

It was early still, still smelling of night. Mistiness and coolness touched our faces; there were long lengths of sun and shadow on the road. Mother and Father, Susie and I walked along the pavement.

'Lift me up on your soldier,' I asked my father, and he smiled and hoisted me up as in Cardiff and carried me a little way so that I could see over hedges. Then, leaving him, three of us walked back to our cottage.

We stood on the pavement, Grandmother just behind us in the doorway's shade, and watched the father, husband, son going from us. He went quickly, not looking back.

He went quickly, and far, and we watched him all the way. At last we saw the small khaki figure stop and turn and wave to us. We waved back, waved, waved, waved. Susie and I called to him, but he didn't hear. Mother held Susie high, then me, and he signalled with his cane and his cap to show that he had seen. The nickel-plate on his military cane glinted in the sun, but no light shone from his cap badge because my father was 287076 Spr WC Dyment RE and the insignia of the Royal Engineers was a dull bronze.

We expected him to stand there for a long time, waving to us, and were surprised when he suddenly spun round and walked away. A hedge partly screened him from us. There were trees now and the hedge got higher and soon there was nothing of him but his cap above the hedge bobbing with his stride as a rider goes up and down with his horse. The cap receded, getting smaller and more indistinct, until we didn't know whether we were seeing his cap or the leaves of trees. Susie and I continued to stare, hoping it was his cap. Mother continued to stare, too, at the empty hedge and fields. And neither Susie nor I noticed her go in again, she went so quietly.

On Active Service with the British Expeditionary Force

My own dearest wife and children and Mother,

Thank you so much, my dear, for your two letters. I have not had time to answer them till now, though I wanted to badly, thinking of you all day as I do. Your letters are very welcome to me. They make this life out here a little more endurable. Please write as often as you can.

I was sorry to hear that the children have not been well. You did quite right in telling me. Please do not keep anything back from me because you think it would hurt me to know. If you do not tell me of these unhappy things, I shall only suspect them, imagine terrible illnesses and difficulties about which you keep silent for my sake. I shall worry like that. So please tell me all.

I am glad both the children are better now. It must be awfully trying for you having to deal all by yourself with the children. I wish Clifford did not cry so much – I do not know what on earth to suggest to keep him quiet. I fear he looks like developing into a troublesome child. And then on top of all this there is the housework and the shopping. That must be difficult with rationing, I know. You mention being short of sweet things for the kiddies. You will remember we used to find Lyle's Golden Syrup good, but I suppose it is as hard to obtain now as sugar. I shall be glad of the day when I am back in Caerleon to help you. But there does not seem much chance of that at present. The leave I mentioned in my earlier letters as being likely has been cancelled. Twice that has happened already. Truly, my luck seems at the bottom of the sea.

I must stop now. Forgive the gloomy tone of the last sentence – life is as pleasant as it can be here on the whole, but I was so looking forward to leave. Write to me soon, dear. How is Grandmother? I hope her heart is not giving her too much trouble? Perhaps you might be able to get in a bottle of brandy? It would do her the world of good, I think, when she is not feeling well. Tell her to write to me. I want to hear from her. My love to Clifford and Susie, and many, many kisses for you, my darling wife.

Your affectionate
WILL

P.S.   It was good of you to send the photo as I asked – it helps me so much to see you, if only on a picture. God bless you.

My dearest wife and children,

Your parcel came this morning. Thank you for putting so many good things in it. It was well packed. Only the rather crumbly shortbread was broken. The ointment I find good, but the powder is useless – the lice gobble it up. They grow fat on it. You can almost see the loathsome creatures squatting back on their heels and laughing. But the ointment *kills* them. Lice here are as big as rabbits. I've heard that Boots the chemists sell some good stuff that you put in the seams of your clothes and it keeps the vermin away. It's about 1/–a tube. Perhaps you could inquire about it some time?

Well dear, this isn't a very beautiful letter, I am afraid – but out here sordid facts cannot be avoided. But this is really only a note to tell you I had the parcel and to thank you for it, and to send my love to you and mother and the kiddies.

Good night, my dear. Kiss the children good night for me.

Your affectionate

WILL

P.S.   George sent me a parcel a little time ago. Some cake she had made, and a dozen of her lemon curd tarts – she knows how I like them. She makes them like nobody else in the world. I am writing to thank her this afternoon.

My own dearest wife and children,

I am scribbling this in a few moments I have after breakfast, sitting in the sunshine on some sandbags. I just wanted to let you know, my dear, that I have heard there is a good chance of leave soon – any time now. Do you know, we have 14 days leave now from leaving London till the day we report back there – that is, 13 clear days. I hope they will not alter this arrangement by the time I get my leave! Real Dyment luck that would be!

I want to come dearly to see you, darling, and yet I feel I shall be unhappy when I do because I shall be thinking all the time of going back. Going back is a bitter thought in the heaven of being with you, my dear one. Sometimes I feel I would rather stay out here with no leaves at all until the whole terrible business is over – and then come home to stay for good. What a wonderful day that will be!

Will you tell me what the children would like for presents when I come? If this leave materialises, I mean. You see, I may be able to come home suddenly, and I would like to know of something they would be fond of that I could bring them. I should not like to bring presents that would be a disappointment to them. I could buy their presents – and one for you, my darling! – while I am waiting at Paddington for the train.

Excuse this bad writing – I'm writing on my knee with a bit of blue lead that needs sharpening. Looking forward to your letters.

Your affectionate

WILL

NOTHING IS TO BE WRITTEN ON THIS SIDE EXCEPT THE DATE AND THE SIGNATURE OF THE SENDER. SENTENCES NOT REQUIRED MAY BE ERASED. IF ANYTHING ELSE IS ADDED THE POSTCARD WILL BE DESTROYED. POSTAGE MUST BE PREPAID ON ANY LETTER OR POSTCARD ADDRESSED TO THE SENDER OF THIS CARD.

I AM QUITE WELL

~~I HAVE BEEN ADMITTED INTO HOSPITAL~~

~~SICK~~ ~~AND AM GOING ON WELL~~

~~WOUNDED~~ ~~AND HOPE TO BE DISCHARGED SOON~~

~~I AM BEING SENT DOWN TO THE BASE~~

LETTER DATED *Sept. 27th*

I HAVE RECEIVED YOUR ~~TELEGRAM DATED~~

~~PARCEL DATED~~

LETTER FOLLOWS AT FIRST OPPORTUNITY

I HAVE RECEIVED NO LETTER FROM YOU

~~LATELY~~

FOR A LONG TIME

SIGNATURE ONLY *W Dyment*

DATE: *12.10.17*

My dearest wife and children,

A short letter this, my dearest, dashed off in an odd spare moment, written on my knee out of doors. I have had nothing from you for days – I am a bit worried – I feel I must write to you – I am longing to be with you tonight. The sun has gone down, and I can smell apples. It reminds me of the evening we talked so long in your father's garden, among the fruit trees. So many things like this remind me of you. A thousand times a day.

Your affectionate
WILL

My dearest wife,

Thank you for your long letter. I was very amused at what you wrote about the children's prayers, how when you were teaching them to say 'Feed the young and tender plant' Clifford shouted 'That's me!' and when you came to 'Give us this day our daily bread' Susie chimed in with '*And* treacle'. That will make me chuckle for days. You are able to get Lyle's G.S. then. Good.

I am sorry about you not having letters from me. Perhaps by now you will have heard, because I *have* written. Remember, when the postwoman walks straight by our door, as you say she has done lately, it doesn't mean I have not written. It is simply that sometimes my letters to you are held up as yours are to me sometimes. So there is no need for your heart to sink when you see the postwoman pass our house, my dear. I hope you get this letter soon. You will probably get it. with several of my earlier letters at the same time – just as I received *two* letters of yours. Write soon, dearest.

Your affectionate
WILL

P.S.   There is no need to be anxious about me, dear. Really, I am very comfortable in this new job, which is just right for me. It is so much better than where I was before, in the support lines. It is very quiet here.

Dear Mrs Dyment,

It is my unpleasant duty to have to write and tell you that your husband has been killed in action. The only consolation was that he died instantly and without any pain. We were being shelled at H.Q. and he was mending my table when a piece of shell hit him on the head and killed him instantly. We all feel his loss tremendously, from the General downwards we thought the world of him, he was such a splendid fellow, always cheerful, a lion for work and a good friend to everyone he came in contact with. I feel his loss as keenly as I would that of a brother officer. If everyone would carry on as he did we should feel the world was a better place to live in. I know how you and his kiddies will feel it but you will I know be a little consoled to know that we all thought him just as fine a fellow as you did.

Needless to say his funeral was as solemn as it could be out here. His grave is well behind the line and a cross will be erected.

If there is anything I can do or tell you please don't hesitate to write to me. My address is the same as your late husband's.

Yours sincerely,
W O Rushton
Captain

Paul Bailey

'The Professor'

From *An Immaculate Mistake*

Paul Bailey was nicknamed 'The Professor' as a boy by his parents, who considered that he had 'more brains than were good for him'. They were bewidered by his love of reading and acting; and his homosexuality and his writing ambitions were also strange to their understanding of life. But they were proud and encouraging, as these extracts show.

Nicholas Nickleby

'Here's a big fat book for you, son. It's by old Charlie Dickens. He hadn't been long gone from the world when I was just a nipper.'

It was a very fat book, the fattest I had ever seen, fatter even than the Bible.

'"That will do for my boy," I said to the woman who was throwing it out. "He'll put it to good use."'

The book my father had rescued for me was *Nicholas Nickleby*. It smelt mouldy, and its pages had turned yellow.

'Don't turn your nose up at it, son. I know it's seen better days, but the words are the same ones Charlie wrote, and that's what matters.'

I placed *Nicholas Nickleby* on the kitchen table, because it was far too heavy to hold. I studied every one of the drawings inside, in the order they appeared – starting with 'Mr Ralph Nickleby's First Visit to his Poor Relations' and ending with 'The Children at their

Cousin's Grave'. Mr Ralph Nickleby seemed to be very angry at having to visit his poor relations, who didn't look at all poor to me – the women had on long dresses that weren't torn, and the man was quite smart in his funny coat with the two bits hanging down the back that my father told me were called 'tails'. I didn't think they looked as poor as the gypsies on the other side of the street, who went off to Kent for their holidays to pick hops.

'There's poor, and then there's poor,' said my mother, from the stove. 'If I've told you once, I've told you a thousand times – being poor doesn't mean being scruffy. Don't judge people by the likes of *them*.'

I asked my father if Nicholas was real.

'No, son. He'd be make-believe, wouldn't he? Out of Charlie's head.'

That evening, when supper was over and the dishes washed, my father and I were banished to the front room. He had promised to read to me from the 'dust trap', and my mother wanted to listen to some nice music on the wireless.

He began at the beginning.

' "There once lived, in a –" '

He cleared his throat, and began again.

' "There once lived, in a –" ' He gulped. ' "– in Devonshire, one Mr Godfrey Nickleby . . ." '

(Four years after his death, when I put *Nicholas Nickleby* to the 'good use' he had predicted, I realised why he had cleared his throat, why he had gulped, why he had been embarrassed – it was the word 'sequestered' in the novel's opening sentence: 'There once lived, in a sequestered part of the county of Devonshire, one Mr Godfrey Nickleby . . .' 'Sequestered' was totally foreign to him. He'd never had cause to say 'sequestered'. The sight of it on the page had upset him, briefly; had made him keenly aware of his ignorance. The cough and the gulp were his camouflage for that hated 'sequestered'.)

My mother disapproved of *Nicholas Nickleby*. It was a book with a Past – it had been in other hands, and God alone knew whose hands they were. It was old, and it gave off a nasty smell. Its days, in her view, were numbered.

'I can't think what possessed your father to bring it into the house.'

'He brought it home for me.'

'Then why don't you repay him and read it, instead of leaving it about the place to gather dust?'

'I will read it. One day.'

I was fifteen when the day came. I opened *Nicholas Nickleby*, and closed it shut within the hour.

'I have some good news for you,' I told my mother.

'Your good news is usually my bad. What is it now?'

'You can throw this away.' I handed her the 'dust trap'.

'I shall do no such thing. Your father brought that home for you.'

'I'm going to have to borrow it from the library,' I said, teasing her. Then I explained why. 'There are pages missing. Dozens of them.'

'Your dad was not to know.' The sharpness had left her voice. 'The woman didn't say. He thought it would make you happy. He wasn't to know it wouldn't.'

(Watching *Nicholas Nickleby* in the theatre, in 1980, when I was forty-three, I found myself in tears. I remembered my father giving me the book, I remembered 'sequestered', I remembered rushing off to the library on Lavender Hill to get another, complete, copy, and the joy of finding one on the shelves.)

The Duchess of Marlborough

'Did I hear you aright or am I dreaming? You're going to play *who*?'

'The Duchess of Marlborough, Mum. Sarah, Duchess of Marlborough.'

'But she's a woman.'

'Of course she is. She was, I mean. She's been dead a long time.'

'And she's the part you've been asked to play?'

'I had to audition for it. It's the leading role. The producer found me the best.'

'Did he now? Best is as best does, and you haven't done it yet. What about the Duke?'

'What about him?'

'Well, couldn't you play him?'

'I don't want to. He doesn't have much to say. He's only a minor character. Sarah's the leading role.'

'Tell me again and I might believe you. I dread to think what your poor father would have thought, I really do. Will you be wearing clothes?'

I did not understand her question, and said so.

'Women's clothes is what I'm getting at.'

'Yes, Mum. How can I pretend to be a woman if I'm not wearing women's clothes?'

'It's no use asking me. I'm no expert, I'm sure. A son of mine a duchess! It sounds all funny to me.'

In Shakespeare's time, I said, when women were forbidden to act in public, the female characters were always played by boys. The first Juliet was a boy, and the first Ophelia, and the first Lady Macbeth.

She thanked me for the history lesson, and advised me to come down out of the clouds, because I would never be able to learn my duchess's lines if I stayed up there.

Viceroy Sarah, written by Norman Ginsbury in the 1930s as a vehicle for Edith Evans, was a virtually forgotten piece when we performed it in December 1950. Our producer, the senior English teacher, had chosen it because the school was celebrating its two-hundred-and-fiftieth anniversary, and a play that dealt with the machinations at the court of Queen Anne seemed appropriate. Our founder, being a baronet, would have had audience with her.

The course of my life was changed as a result of playing Sarah. Assuming her personality, I knew the power of artifice. For three memorable winter nights, I said goodbye to my dull self and became that creature of violent contrasts. I stormed; I screamed; I even shed real tears. I told the Queen what was good for her, and treated the wily Abigail Hill with suspicion – my involvement with Sarah was total. In costume, wig, and make-up, I was a forceful woman of the world. Acting, I understood, was a release into the nature of others. It was a wonderful way of not being Peter.

'You can keep your tantrums for the stage' became my mother's newest expression. 'Viceroy Sarah's got no place in my kitchen, putting on airs.'

She came to the opening performance. When it was over, she accepted the congratulations due to the mother of the brilliant star with a lack of surprise that disconcerted the parents of friends: 'It was no more than I expected,' she observed nonchalantly.

Before I went to bed that night, I made my customary mistake of asking for her opinion: 'What was I like?'

'You weren't like the others. They were more like themselves. They were more natural.'

I decoded this, in my need for her approval, as praise. Perhaps she was telling me, in a circuitous fashion, that I had succeeded in becoming the Duchess of Marlborough.

Perhaps

The following December, I was the leading lady again, and rapturously happy to be free from myself.

'Emma, did you say? Emma who?'

'Emma Woodhouse.'

'Who's she when she's out?'

(This was one of my mother's favourite rhetorical questions. Only now, writing it down, am I drawn to translate it. By 'out' she meant, I think, 'out of the lunatic asylum'. Another much-used phrase was 'There are more out than in', which suggested that there were mad people walking the streets who, in her view, should have been locked up, for their own good. It followed that any woman I had been invited to play must be slightly peculiar, at least. That Emma Woodhouse, like that Viceroy Sarah, was different from the rest of us.)

She saw me as Emma, in that creaky adaptation of Jane Austen's masterpiece, and said I came over as a 'bossy cow'.

'Thank you.'

'If I'd been that Harriet Smith, I'd have soon pulled her down a peg or two. I would have stood up for myself and told her to mind her own bloody business. I can't abide interferers.'

'Yes, Mum.'

'You just make sure you don't bring any of her behaviour back home with you.'

'You're playing *who*?'

'King Henry IV.'

'A man?'

'Of course.'

'Well, that's an improvement.'

(I had wanted to play Hotspur, but the producer insisted that the King would make greater demands on my talent. 'But he just sits on his throne and moans,' I complained. I was assured that he had reasons for moaning, which I would discover in rehearsal. I did.)

I wore a robe instead of a dress, and had a grey beard stuck to my chin with glue.

My mother said she preferred me as Sarah and Emma, for all that I was being a man at last. A person could catch the drift of what they were talking about, whereas that King went on and on and on.

'I can't help it,' she confessed. 'It's exactly the same with that closet music when it comes on the wireless. All those words give me a headache. That's Shakespeare's trouble, if you ask me – words.'

J B Priestley

Three Delights

From *Delight*

The dedication in Delight *is:*

> FOR THE FAMILY
> *These small amends*
> *With the old monster's love.*

The preface is sub-titled 'Or The Grumbler's Apology', and he begins:

I have always been a grumbler. All the records going back to earliest childhood establish this fact. Probably I arrived here a malcontent, convinced I had been sent to the wrong planet.

He goes on:

I have grumbled all over the world, across seas, on mountains, in deserts. I have grumbled as much at home as abroad, and so I have been the despair of my womenfolk. If, for example, an hotel gives me a bad breakfast, I have only to grumble away for a few minutes to feel that some reasonable balance has been restored: the grumble has been substracted from the badness of the breakfast. So it is no use crying to me 'Oh – do be quiet! It's bad enough without your grumbling.' My mind does not move along these lines. If I have not had a good breakfast, I argue, at least I have had a good grumble. Thus I have always been innocent of the major charge – that of trying deliberately to make things worse.

So here is Delight. *The preface ends*:

So many a decent fellow, showing a better face to his bad luck than ever I appear to have shown to my good luck, must have cried in his exasperation: 'Does this chap never enjoy anything?' And my reply, long overdue, is this book . . . I have kept close to this little book on *Delight*, so that it could be my apology, my bit of penitence, for having grumbled so much, for having darkened the breakfast table, almost ruined the lunch, nearly silenced the dinner party, for all the fretting and chafing, grousing and croaking, for the old glum look and the thrust-out lower lip. So, my long-suffering kinsfolk, my patient friends, may a glimmer of that delight which has so often possessed me, but perhaps too frequently in secret, now reach you from these pages.

Here are three of them:

Seventeen

When I was a boy I lived in a new suburb with playing fields not far away. During the holidays we would pick sides for football, always soccer, and play all day. We might have different meal-times – rushing home to dinner any time between twelve and two – but this only made the daylong game easier to manage. We would arrive home, breathless and scarlet, put away two or three helpings of suet pudding, and then hurry back to the game. (Am I suffering for it now, in middle-age? I doubt it. And as for most of the others, they never reached their middle twenties but died among the shell holes and barbed wire on July 1st, 1916). In the morning, in the afternoon, in the early evening, as I went clattering in my football boots, past the row of half-built houses towards the field, I would hear the *thud-thud-thud* of the ball, a sound unlike any other, and delight would rise in my heart. There are moments even now, forty years afterwards, when I find myself in some country lane and hear that *thud-thud-thud*, that unmistakable call to the field, and I feel an itching in my insteps and for a daft fraction of a second I imagine the game is still there for me to join, forgetting how the years have gone and that I am now a heavy ageing man. But before the tide of regret sweeps over my mind, the grey and salty tide, there sparkles, like some treasure on the sand, not some mere memory of past pleasure but, for a flashing quarter-second, the old delight itself.

Forty-seven

There was a time when merely wearing long trousers brought me delight. In those days, when I must have been about fifteen, I had only one suit – my best – with long trousers. My other suits had knee-breeches, buttoning tightly just below the knee and worn with thick long stockings, turned down at the top. There was really nothing wrong with my appearance when I wore these knee-breeches and long stockings, for after years of football I had muscular well-shaped legs; but whenever I wore them I felt I was still imprisoned, a shamefaced giant, in the stale miniature world of childhood. Condemned – and I use this term because there were strict rules at home about which suits could be worn – to wear these knee-breeches, I felt that no glimpse of my real self could catch the town's eye: I might almost have been sent to school in a pram. Conversely I felt that as soon as I put on the long trousers then appearance and reality were gloriously one; I joined the world of men; and even without doing anything more than wear these trousers – and leaving the other wretched things at home – I could feel my whole nature expanding magnificently. On the occasional days when I was allowed to wear the adult trousers to go to school, I almost floated there. Never did eighteen inches of cloth do more for the human spirit. On those mornings now when I seem to stare sullenly at the wreck of a shining world, why do I not remind myself that although I grow old and fat and peevish *at least I am wearing my long trousers?*

Sixty-three

One of the delights known to age and beyond the grasp of youth is that of *Not Going*. When we are young it is almost agony not to go. We feel we are being left out of life, that the whole wonderful procession is sweeping by, probably for ever, while we are weeping or sulking behind bars. Not to have an invitation – for the dance, the party, the match, the picnic, the excursion, the gang on holiday – is to be diminished, perhaps kept at midget's height for years. To have an invitation and then not to be able to go – oh cursed spite! Thus we torment ourselves in the April of our time. Now in my early November not only do I not care the rottenest fig whether I receive an invitation or not, but after having carelessly accepted the invitation I can find delight in knowing that I am *Not Going*. I arrived at this by two stages. At the first, after years of illusion, I finally decided I was missing nothing by not going. Now, at the second and, I hope, final stage, I stay away and no longer care whether I am missing anything or not. But don't I like to enjoy myself? On the contrary, by Not Going, that is just what I am trying to do.

William Cooper

Scenes . . .

From *From Early Life*

People born around the turn of the century will remember the first planes, the last horse-drawn vehicles. Here are two of William Cooper's recollections of his childhood in that different world 80 years ago.

Though the classrooms were disciplined and quiet, the playground was noisy and rough, of course. We played wildly chasing games of Tick; and kicked a ball about, dribbling and shooting in mimicry of Association Football. (I don't think I even heard of Rugby football until a good ten years later.) On the other hand there was a popular vogue for playing marbles, introducing an element of the sedate. I had a collection of polished stone marbles of different colours; grey, greenish, bluish, reddish; and – the treasures of the collection – some glass 'ollies', beautiful spheres of clear glass in which were embedded curving streaks of bright colour. (Also some inferior moulded green glass specimens which came out of the pinched necks of 'pop' bottles, specimens won from inferior boys and not collected by me – class distinction starts in the cradle.) We played the game which I gather is still played in some form or other today. A chalked ring up to which one rolls one's marble in order to land it in the ring or knock other boys' marbles out of the ring. A more aggressive technique than rolling was shooting: one lightly clenched one's fist with the thumb trapped between the first and second finger, rested the marble against one's thumb-nail, and then sprang the trap – the marble shot out with deadly effect.

However, the game I favoured most for a spell had a strong 'entrepreneurial' (called thus in order to be in accord with recent improvements in the use of our language) element. It must be the only time I've ever favoured the 'entrepreneurial' element in anything – entrepreneurs, ceaselessly at the ready to take advantage of anyone giving the slightest opening, inevitably strike me as Nature's barrow-boys. For this game one equipped oneself with a piece of wood some eighteen inches long and six inches high, from the lower edge of which one carved out half a dozen marble-width slots, inscribing above them the numbers 1 to 6, taking care to put the high numbers at the ends. One squatted beside the playground wall, set up one's board, and invited all and sundry to roll up their marbles through the slots – paying out the number of marbles inscribed above the slot if a marble went through, confiscating the marble if it didn't. I made a fortune (in marbles). If a boy appeared who was too expert, one simply picked up one's board and went away for a while.

Yet more surprising to me than the recollection of my making a fortune even in marbles is a clear image of my playing marbles along the gutter below the edge of the pavement. It would be suicidal now, yet I'm sure I did it. So sparse and so slow-moving was the traffic, mostly horse-drawn, seventy years ago.

Cigarette cards. In those days every cigarette manu-facturer enclosed in each packet of cigarettes a little pasteboard card with a coloured picture on it. The picture was one of a series – of soldiers in different uniforms, characters from Dickens, British butterflies . . . The cards in each series were numbered, and one's aim was to collect a complete set. As my father smoked so much I had a good start in accumulating a supply of cards from Gold Flake – W. D. & H. O. Wills. Other boys collected, and in a quiet corner of the playground a busy exchange took place in cards of which one had more than one for cards one lacked to make up the set. I don't know if it was the result of the manufacturers artfully printing smaller numbers of some particular cards – in the present day, it could certainly be so, so as to make boys pester their fathers to buy more cigarettes – but in any series there always seemed to be two or three numbers that were rarer than the rest.

The idea was to collect a complete set in pristine condition. With cards that were soiled one played a game, a game of acquisition. Each player held a card horizontally between his forefinger and middle finger and then, with a flick of his wrist, sent it skimming through the air to a chosen spot on the ground; where, if it didn't cover any of the cards already there, it remained; but, if it did cover one of the cards already there, its owner scooped the lot.

But my recollection of cigarette cards is not without significance beyond itself – and I'm not occupying my mind with trifles such as the Freudian significance of collecting, but with something more significant to me. The small cards I have been remembering so far came out of packets of 10 or 20 cigarettes. Boxes of 100 cigarettes contained large cards, and my father some-times bought, to my mother's disapproval, his supplies by the hundred. There was one series of large cards showing beautiful reproductions of the crests of Oxford and Cambridge Colleges. I fell in love with them. I can still see, for instance, the perfect disposition and colour of the cardinals' hats in the crest of Christ Church, Oxford.

Somewhere along the line of my remembering I've got to try and locate the genesis of my unheard-of intention of going to Oxford or Cambridge University *myself*. Could the seed of that intention to go to one of the Colleges have been sown, when I was nine, ten, eleven . . . by a beautiful cigarette card?

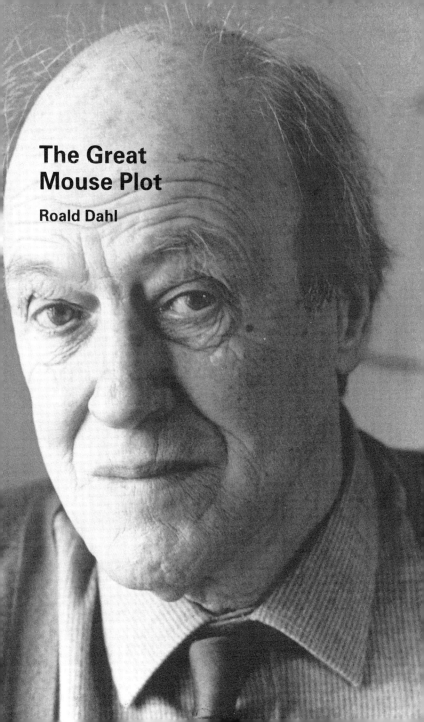

The Great
Mouse Plot

Roald Dahl

Roald Dahl

The Great Mouse Plot

From *Boy*

This plot is one of the vivid details of Roald Dahl's childhood.

Mrs Pratchett

The sweet-shop in Llandaff in the year 1923 was the very centre of our lives. To us, it was what a bar is to a drunk, or a church is to a Bishop. Without it, there would have been little to live for. But it had one terrible drawback, this sweet-shop. The woman who owned it was a horror. We hated her and we had good reason for doing so.

Her name was Mrs Pratchett. She was a small skinny old hag with a moustache on her upper lip and a mouth as sour as a green gooseberry. She never smiled. She never welcomed us when we went in, and the only times she spoke were when she said things like, 'I'm watchin' you so keep yer thievin' fingers off them chocolates!' Or 'I don't want you in 'ere just to look around! Either you *forks* out or you *gets* out!'

But by far the most loathsome thing about Mrs Pratchett was the filth that clung around her. Her apron was grey and greasy. Her blouse had bits of breakfast all over it, toast-crumbs and tea stains and splotches of dried egg-yolk. It was her hands, however, that disturbed us most. They were disgusting. They were black with dirt and grime. They looked as though they had been putting lumps of coal on the fire all day long. And do not forget please that it was these very hands and fingers that she plunged into the sweet-jars when we asked for a pennyworth of Treacle Toffee or Wine Gums or Nut Clusters or whatever. There were precious few health laws in those days, and nobody, least of all Mrs Pratchett, ever thought of using a little shovel for getting out the sweets as they do today. The mere sight of her grimy right hand with its black fingernails digging an ounce of Chocolate Fudge out of a jar would have caused a starving tramp to go running from the shop. But not us. Sweets were our life-blood. We would have put up with far worse than that to get them. So we simply stood and watched in sullen silence while this disgusting old woman stirred around inside the jars with her foul fingers.

The other thing we hated Mrs Pratchett for was her meanness. Unless you spent a whole sixpence all in one go, she wouldn't give you a bag. Instead you got your sweets twisted up in a small piece of newspaper which she tore off a pile of old *Daily Mirrors* lying on the counter.

So you can well understand that we had it in for Mrs Pratchett in a big way, but we didn't quite know what to do about it. Many schemes were put forward but none of them was any good. None of them, that is, until suddenly, one memorable afternoon, we found the dead mouse.

The Great Mouse Plot

My four friends and I had come across a loose floor-board at the back of the classroom, and when we prised it up with the blade of a pocket-knife, we discovered a big hollow space underneath. This, we decided, would be our secret hiding place for sweets and other small treasures such as conkers and monkey-nuts and birds' eggs. Every afternoon, when the last lesson was over, the five of us would wait until the classroom had emptied, then we would lift up the floor-board and examine our secret hoard, perhaps adding to it or taking something away.

One day, when we lifted it up, we found a dead mouse lying among our treasures. It was an exciting discovery. Thwaites took it out by its tail and waved it in front of our faces. 'What shall we do with it?' he cried.

'It stinks!' someone shouted. 'Throw it out of the window quick!'

'Hold on a tick,' I said. 'Don't throw it away.'

Thwaites hesitated. They all looked at me.

When writing about oneself, one must strive to be truthful. Truth is more important than modesty. I must tell you, therefore, that it was I and I alone who had the idea for the great and daring Mouse Plot. We all have our moments of brilliance and glory, and this was mine.

'Why don't we', I said, 'slip it into one of Mrs Pratchett's jars of sweets? Then when she puts her dirty hand in to grab a handful, she'll grab a stinky dead mouse instead.'

The other four stared at me in wonder. Then, as the sheer genius of the plot began to sink in, they all started grinning. They slapped me on the back. They cheered me and danced around the classroom. 'We'll do it today!' they cried. 'We'll do it on the way home! *You* had the idea,' they said to me, 'so *you* can be the one to put the mouse in the jar.'

Thwaites handed me the mouse. I put it into my trouser pocket. Then the five of us left the school, crossed the village green and headed for the sweep-shop. We were tremendously jazzed up. We felt like a gang of desperados setting out to rob a train or blow up the sheriff's office.

'Make sure you put it into a jar which is used often,' somebody said.

'I'm putting it in Gobstoppers,' I said. 'The Gobstopper jar is never behind thc counter.'

'I've got a penny,' Thwaites said, 'so I'll ask for one Sherbet Sucker and one Bootlace. And while she turns away to get them, you slip the mouse in quickly with the Gobstoppers.'

Thus everything was arranged. We were strutting a little as we entered the shop. We were the victors now and Mrs Pratchett was the victim. Shc stood behind the counter, and her small malignant pig-eyes watched us suspiciously as we came forward.

'One Sherbet Sucker, please,' Thwaites said to her, holding out his penny.

I kept to the rear of the group, and when I saw Mrs Pratchett turn her head away for a couple of seconds to fish a Sherbet Sucker out of the box, I lifted the heavy glass lid of the Gobstopper jar and dropped the mouse in. Then I replaced the lid as silently as possible. My heart was thumping like mad and my hands had gone all sweaty.

'And one Bootlace, please,' I heard Thwaites saying. When I turned round, I saw Mrs Pratchett holding out the Bootlace in her filthy fingers.

'I don't want all the lot of you troopin' in 'ere if only one of you is buyin',' she screamed at us. 'Now beat it! Go on, get out!'

As soon as we were outside, we broke into a run. 'Did you do it?' they shouted at me.

'Of course I did!' I said.

'Well done you!' they cried. 'What a super show!'

I felt like a hero. I *was* a hero. It was marvellous to be so popular.

Mr Coombes

The flush of triumph over the dead mouse was carried forward to the next morning as we all met again to walk to school.

'Let's go in and see if it's still in the jar,' somebody said as we approached the sweet-shop.

'Don't,' Thwaites said firmly. 'It's too dangerous. Walk past as though nothing has happened.'

As we came level with the shop we saw a cardboard notice hanging on the door. CLOSED. We stopped and stared. We had never known the sweet-shop to be closed at this time in the morning, even on Sundays.

'What's happened?' we asked each other. 'What's going on?'

We pressed our faces against the window and looked inside. Mrs Pratchett was nowhere to be seen.

'Look!' I cried. 'The Gobstopper jar's gone! It's not on the shelf! There's a gap where it used to be!'

'It's on the floor!' someone said. 'It's smashed to bits and there's Gobstoppers everywhere!'

'There's the mouse!' someone else shouted.

We could see it all, the huge glass jar smashed to smithereens with the dead mouse lying in the wreckage and hundreds of many-coloured Gobstoppers littering the floor.

'She got such a shock when she grabbed hold of the mouse that she dropped everything,' somebody was saying.

'But why didn't she sweep it all up and open the shop?' I asked.

Nobody answered me.

We turned away and walked towards the school. All of a sudden we had begun to feel slightly uncomfortable. There was something not quite right about the shop being closed. Even Thwaites was unable to offer a reasonable explanation. We became silent. There was a faint scent of danger in the air now. Each one of us had caught a whiff of it. Alarm bells were beginning to ring faintly in our ears.

After a while, Thwaites broke the silence. 'She must have got one heck of a shock,' he said. He paused. We all looked at him, wondering what wisdom the great medical authority was going to come out with next.

'After all,' he went on, 'to catch hold of a dead mouse when you're expecting to catch hold of a Gobstopper must be a pretty frightening experience. Don't you agree?'

Nobody answered him.

'Well now,' Thwaites went on, 'when an old person like Mrs Pratchett suddenly gets a very big shock, I suppose you know what happens next?'

'What?' we said. 'What happens?'

'You ask my father,' Thwaites said. 'He'll tell you.'

'You tell us,' we said.

'It gives her a heart attack,' Thwaites announced. 'Her heart stops beating and she's dead in five seconds.'

For a moment or two my own heart stopped beating. Thwaites pointed a finger at me and said darkly, 'I'm afraid you've killed her.'

'*Me*?' I cried. 'Why just *me*?'

'It was *your* idea,' he said. 'And what's more, *you* put the mouse in.'

All of a sudden, I was a murderer.

At exactly that point, we heard the school bell ringing in the distance and we had to gallop the rest of the way so as not to be late for prayers.

Prayers were held in the Assembly Hall. We all perched in rows on wooden benches while the teachers sat up on the platform in armchairs, facing us. The five of us scrambled into our places just as the Headmaster marched in, followed by the rest of the staff.

The Headmaster is the only teacher at Llandaff Cathedral School that I can remember, and for a reason you will soon discover, I can remember him very clearly indeed. His name was Mr Coombes and I have a picture in my mind of a giant of a man with a face like a ham and a mass of rusty-coloured hair that sprouted in a tangle all over the top of his head. All grown-ups appear as giants to small children. But Headmasters (and policemen) are the biggest giants of all and acquire a marvellously exaggerated stature. It is possible that Mr Coombes was a perfectly normal being, but in my memory he was a giant, a tweed-suited giant who always wore a black gown over his tweeds and a waist-coat under his jacket.

Mr Coombes now proceeded to mumble through the same old prayers we had every day, but this morning, when the last amen had been spoken, he did not turn and lead his group rapidly out of the Hall as usual. He remained standing before us, and it was clear he had an announcement to make.

'The whole school is to go out and line up around the playground immediately,' he said. 'Leave your books behind. And no talking.'

Mr Coombes was looking grim. His hammy pink face had taken on that dangerous scowl which only appeared when he was extremely cross and somebody was for the high-jump. I sat there small and frightened among the rows and rows of other boys, and to me at that moment the Headmaster, with his black gown draped over his shoulders, was like a judge at a murder trial.

'He's after the killer,' Thwaites whispered to me.

I began to shiver.

'I'll bet the police are here already,' Thwaites went on. 'And the Black Maria's waiting outside.'

As we made our way out to the playground, my whole stomach began to feel as though it was slowly filling up with swirling water. *I am only eight years old,* I told myself. *No little boy of eight has ever murdered anyone. It's not possible.*

Out in the playground on this warm cloudy September morning, the Deputy Headmaster was shouting, 'Line up in forms! Sixth Form over there! Fifth Form next to them! Spread out! Spread out! Get on with it! Stop talking all of you!'

Thwaites and I and my other three friends were in the Second Form, the lowest but one, and we lined up against the red-brick wall of the playground shoulder to shoulder. I can remember that when every boy in the school was in his place, the line stretched right round the four sides of the playground – about one hundred small boys altogether, aged between six and twelve, all of us wearing identical grey shorts and grey blazers and grey stockings and black shoes.

'Stop that *talking*!' shouted the Deputy Head. 'I want absolute silence!'

But why for heaven's sake were we in the playground at all? I wondered. And why were we lined up like this? It had never happened before.

I half-expected to see two policemen come bounding out of the school to grab me by the arms and put handcuffs on my wrists.

A single door led out from the school on to the playground. Suddenly it swung open and through it, like the angel of death, strode Mr Coombes, huge and bulky in his tweed suit and black gown, and beside him, believe it or not, right beside him trotted the tiny figure of Mrs Pratchett herself!

Mrs Pratchett was alive!

The relief was tremendous.

'She's alive! I whispered to Thwaites standing next to me. 'I didn't kill her!' Thwaites ignored me.

'We'll start over here,' Mr Coombes was saying to Mrs Pratchett. He grasped her by one of her skinny arms and led her over to where the Sixth Form was standing. Then, still keeping hold of her arm, he proceeded to lead her at a brisk walk down the line of boys. It was like someone inspecting the troops.

'What on earth are they doing?' I whispered.

Thwaites didn't answer me. I glanced at him. He had gone rather pale.

'Too big,' I heard Mrs Pratchett saying. 'Much too big. It's none of this lot. Let's 'ave a look at some of them titchy ones.'

Mr Coombes increased his pace. 'We'd better go all the way round,' he said. He seemed in a hurry to get it over with now and I could see Mrs Pratchett's skinny goat's legs trotting to keep up with him. They had already inspected one side of the playground where the Sixth Form and half the Fifth Form were standing. We watched them moving down the second side . . . then the third side.

'Still too big,' I heard Mrs Pratchett croaking. 'Much too big! Smaller than these! Much smaller! Where's them nasty little ones?'

They were coming closer to us now . . . closer and closer.

They were starting on the fourth side . . .

Every boy in our form was watching Mr Coombes and Mrs Pratchett as they came walking down the line towards us.

'Nasty cheeky lot, these little 'uns!' I heard Mrs Pratchett muttering. 'They comes into my shop and they thinks they can do what they damn well likes!'

Mr Coombes made no reply to this.

'They nick things when I ain't lookin',' she went on. 'They put their grubby 'ands all over everything and they've got no manners. I don't mind girls. I never 'ave no trouble with girls, but boys is 'ideous and 'orrible! I don't 'ave to tell *you* that, 'Eadmaster, do I?'

'These are the smaller ones,' Mr Coombes said.

I could see Mrs Pratchett's piggy little eyes staring hard at the face of each boy she passed.

Suddenly she let out a high-pitched yell and pointed a dirty finger straight at Thwaites. 'That's 'im!' she yelled. 'That's one of 'em! I'd know 'im a mile away, the scummy little bounder!'

The entire school turned to look at Thwaites. 'W-what have *I* done?' he stuttered, appealing to Mr Coombes.

'Shut up,' Mr Coombes said.

Mrs Pratchett's eyes flicked over and settled on my own face. I looked down and studied the black asphalt surface of the playground.

''Ere's another of 'em!' I heard her yelling. 'That one there!' She was pointing at me now.

'You're quite sure?' Mr Coombes said.

'Of course I'm sure!' she cried. 'I never forgets a face, least of all when it's as sly as that! 'Ee's one of 'em all right! There was five altogether! Now where's them other three?'

The other three, as I knew very well, were coming up next.

Mrs Pratchett's face was glimmering with venom as her eyes travelled beyond me down the line.

'There they are!' she cried out, stabbing the air with her finger. "*Im* . . . and '*im* . . . and '*im*! That's the five of 'em all right! We don't need to look no farther than this, 'Eadmaster! They're all 'ere, the nasty dirty little pigs! You've got their names, 'ave you?'

'I've got their names, Mrs Pratchett,' Mr Coombes told her. 'I'm much obliged to you.'

'And I'm much obliged to *you*, 'Eadmaster,' she answered.

As Mr Coombes led her away across the playground, we heard her saying, 'Right in the jar of Gobstoppers it was! A stinkin' dead mouse which I will never forget as long as I live!'

'You have my deepest sympathy,' Mr Coombes was muttering.

'Talk about shocks!' she went on. 'When my fingers caught 'old of that nasty soggy stinkin' dead mouse . . .' Her voice trailed away as Mr Coombes led her quickly through the door into the school building.

Mrs Pratchett's revenge

Our form master came into the classroom with a piece of paper in his hand. 'The following are to report to the Headmaster's study at once,' he said. 'Thwaites . . . Dahl . . .' And then he read out the other three names which I have forgotten.

The five of us stood up and left the room. We didn't speak as we made our way down the long corridor into the Headmaster's private quarters where the dreaded study was situated. Thwaites knocked on the door.

'Enter!'

We sidled in. The room smelled of leather and tobacco. Mr Coombes was standing in the middle of it, dominating everything, a giant of a man if ever there was one, and in his hands he held a long yellow cane which curved round the top like a walking stick.

'I don't want any lies,' he said. 'I know very well you did it and you were all in it together. Line up over there against the bookcase.'

We lined up, Thwaites in front and I, for some reason, at the very back. I was last in the line.

'You,' Mr Coombes said, pointing the cane at Thwaites, 'Come over here.'

Thwaites went forward very slowly.

'Bend over,' Mr Coombes said.

Thwaites bent over. Our eyes were riveted on him. We were hypnotised by it all. We knew, of course, that boys got the cane now and again, but we had never heard of anyone being made to watch.

'Tighter, boy, tighter!' Mr Coombes snapped out. 'Touch the ground!'

Thwaites touched the carpet with the tips of his fingers.

Mr Coombes stood back and took up a firm stance with his legs well apart. I thought how small Thwaites's bottom looked and how very tight it was. Mr Coombes had his eyes focused squarely upon it. He raised the cane high above his shoulder, and as he brought it down, it made a loud swishing sound, and then there was a crack like a pistol shot as it struck Thwaites's bottom.

Little Thwaites seemed to lift about a foot into the air and he yelled 'Ow-w-w-w-w-w-w-w-w-w!' and straightened up like elastic.

''*Arder!*' shrieked a voice from over in the corner.

Now it was our turn to jump. We looked round and there, sitting in one of Mr Coombes's big leather armchairs, was the tiny loathsome figure of Mrs Pratchett! She was bounding up and down with excitement. 'Lay it into 'im!' she was shrieking. 'Let 'im 'ave it! Teach 'im a lesson!'

'Get down, boy!' Mr Coombes ordered. 'And stay down! You get an extra one every time you straighten up!'

'That's tellin' 'im!' shrieked Mrs Pratchett. 'That's tellin' the little blighter!'

I could hardly believe what I was seeing. It was like some awful pantomime. The violence was bad enough, and being made to watch it was even worse, but with Mrs Pratchett in the audience the whole thing became a nightmare.

Swish-crack! went the cane.

'Ow-w-w-w-w!' yelled Thwaites.

''Arder!' shrieked Mrs Pratchett. 'Stitch 'im up! Make it sting! Tickle 'im up good and proper! Warm 'is backside for 'im! Go on, warm it up, 'Eadmaster!'

Thwaites received four strokes, and by gum, they were four real whoppers.

'Next!' snapped Mr Coombes.

Thwaites came hopping past us on his toes, clutching his bottom with both hands and yelling, 'Ow! Ouch! Ouch! Ouch! Owwwww!'

With tremendous reluctance, the next boy sidled forward to his fate. I stood there wishing I hadn't been last in the line. The watching and waiting were probably even greater torture than the event itself.

Mr Coombes's performance the second time was the same as the first. So was Mrs Pratchett's. She kept up her screeching all the way through, exhorting Mr Coombes to greater and still greater efforts, and the awful thing was that he seemed to be responding to her cries. He was like an athlete who is spurred on by the shouts of the crowd in the stands. Whether this was true or not, I was sure of one thing. He wasn't weakening.

My own turn came at last. My mind was swimming and my eyes had gone all blurry as I went forward to bend over. I can remember wishing my mother would suddenly come bursting into the room shouting, 'Stop! How dare you do that to my son!' But she didn't. All I heard was Mrs Pratchett's dreadful high-pitched voice behind me screeching, 'This one's the cheekiest of the bloomin' lot, 'Eadmaster! Make sure you let 'im 'ave it good and strong!'

Mr Coombes did just that. As the first stroke landed and the pistol-crack sounded, I was thrown forward so violently that if my fingers hadn't been touching the carpet, I think I would have fallen flat on my face. As it was, I was able to catch myself on the palms of my hands and keep my balance. At first I heard only the *crack* and felt absolutely nothing at all, but a fraction of a second later the burning sting that flooded across my buttocks was so terrific that all I could do was gasp. I gave a great gushing gasp that emptied my lungs of every breath of air that was in them.

It felt, I promise you, as though someone had laid a red-hot poker against my flesh and was pressing down on it hard.

The second stroke was worse than the first and this was probably because Mr Coombes was well practised and had a splendid aim. He was able, so it seemed, to land the second one almost exactly across the narrow line where the first one had struck. It is bad enough when the cane lands on fresh skin, but when it comes down on bruised and wounded flesh, the agony is unbelievable.

The third one seemed even worse than the second. Whether or not the wily Mr Coombes had chalked the cane beforehand and had thus made an aiming mark on my grey flannel shorts after the first stroke, I do not know. I am inclined to doubt it because he must have known that this was a practice much frowned upon by Headmasters in general in those days. It was not only regarded as unsporting, it was also an admission that you were not an expert at the job.

By the time the fourth stroke was delivered, my entire backside seemed to be going up in flames.

Far away in the distance, I heard Mr Coombes's voice saying, 'Now get out.'

As I limped across the study clutching my buttocks hard with both hands, a cackling sound came from the armchair over in the corner, and then I heard the vinegary voice of Mrs Pratchett saying, 'I am much obliged to you, 'Eadmaster, very much obliged. I don't think we is goin' to see any more stinkin' mice in my Gobstoppers from now on.'

When I returned to the classroom my eyes were wet with tears and everybody stared at me. My bottom hurt when I sat down at my desk.

That evening after supper my three sisters had their baths before me. Then it was my turn, but as I was about to step into the bathtub, I heard a horrified gasp from my mother behind me.

'What's this?' she gasped. 'What's happened to you?' She was staring at my bottom. I myself had not inspected it up to then, but when I twisted my head around and took a look at one of my buttocks, I saw the scarlet stripes and the deep blue bruising in between.

'Who did this? my mother cried. 'Tell me at once!'

In the end I had to tell her the whole story, while my three sisters (aged nine, six and four) stood around in their nighties listening goggle-eyed. My mother heard me out in silence. She asked no questions. She just let me talk, and when I had finished, she said to our nurse, 'You get them into bed, Nanny. I'm going out.'

If I had had the slightest idea of what she was going to do next, I would have tried to stop her, but I hadn't. She went straight downstairs and put on her hat. Then she marched out of the house, down the drive and on to the road. I saw her through my bedroom window as she went out of the gates and turned left, and I remember calling out to her to come back, come back, come back. But she took no notice of me. She was walking very quickly, with her head held high and her body erect, and by the look of things I figured that Mr Coombes was in for a hard time.

About an hour later, my mother returned and came upstairs to kiss us all goodnight. 'I wish you hadn't done that,' I said to her. 'It makes me look silly.'

'They don't beat small children like that where I come from,' she said. 'I won't allow it.'

'What did Mr Coombes say to you, Mama?'

'He told me I was a foreigner and I didn't understand how British schools were run,' she said.

'Did he get ratty with you?'

'Very ratty,' she said. 'He told me that if I didn't like his methods I could take you away.'

'What did you say?'

'I said I would, as soon as the school year is finished. I shall find you an *English* school this time,' she said. 'Your father was right. English schools are the best in the world.'

'Does that mean it'll be a boarding school?' I asked.

'It'll have to be,' she said. 'I'm not quite ready to move the whole family to England yet.'

So I stayed on at Llandaff Cathedral School until the end of the summer term.

Sylvia Haymon

A Day with the Fenners

From *Opposite the Cross Keys*

When Sylvia Haymon was seven, 60 years ago, she went on a visit to the Fenners, the family of Maud Fenner, her nursery-maid. Sylvia's mother knew nothing about the poverty of poor rural people in the 1920's, and she thought Maud's home would be as spic and span as Maud kept the nursery. Far from it!

When I stayed with the Fenners my bed was the old horsehair sofa which was pushed up against the wall dividing their cottage from the derelict one next door, and at night the noise of the rats on the other side of the partition was dreadfully disturbing. What could they find to eat in that empty house . . . what if not me so conveniently to hand? I lay awake straining for the gnawing throught the lath and plaster which would mean they were on their way.

Not frightened for long, though, Sylvia could scarcely believe her luck to be there. A year before, she'd been on a visit for the day . . .

We went down the garden, Mrs Fenner, Maud and I, following a path trodden between tall grasses and poppies, and accompanied on our way by two pairs of butterflies, one pair cabbage, one, small tortoiseshell. Bees swerved about their business, grasshoppers chirped. The grasses tickled my bare legs.

It was a lovely way to go to the lav.

The privies stood in a row at the bottom of the

garden, looking like bathing huts on a shore from which
the sea had long since retreated. The one between the
Fenner's and the Leaches', like the cottage of which it
was a dependency, tottered in a state of dereliction, the
roof stripped of its pantiles, the door hanging by a
single hinge. Under the sagging lintel crowded several
little clay cups of house martins' nests; and it was clear
that a further colony of the birds was housed within, for
the air was busy with the non-stop twitter of nestlings,
and the tireless comings and goings of the parent birds.

When Mrs Fenner opened the door into our own
kingdom I was delighted to discover that one pair,
preferring privacy, it may be, or simply finding standing
room only next door, had taken up residence in an
angle of the Fenner lav. As we entered – all of us
together! What new experience was in store? – a flash of
black and white shot ahead of us like an arrow, and, in
an instant, was on its way out again, back to the insect-
rich outdoors.

The privy doors were not privy at all, beginning some
eighteen inches above the ground, and ending at least
as much below the lintel; in addition to which, each had
an unglazed porthole, the shape of a playing-card club,
gouged out of the centre. You could see that someone
was in the Leaches' lav, which was the only one which
was painted; spick and span like the polished black
shoes and the grey socks with fancy clox which showed
under the door.

'Mr Leach,' said Mrs Fenner, making no effort to
keep her voice down. 'Known him to be there of a
Sunday from dinner till tea.' The black shoes scuffed
each other self-consciously. 'You got to hand it to him,
poor bugger. He do keep trying.'

New smells. Horrible new smells, but with such com-
pensations they might have been flower fragrances. Not

only a nest of real live birds to watch while you were doing your business, but company! Suddenly the whole boring business of evacuation was transformed: a social event, a lav party, as it might be a Christmas or a birthday one, for which you might send out invitations, with spaces to fill in the date and the times, and RSVP at the end. No stupid games like My Friend's Chair and Pin the Tail on the Donkey. Just you and two best friends – there were never more than two people you *really* wanted to invite, the rest were just make-weights, there to make up the numbers – sitting at peace with the world.

There were three holes in the wooden seat at Opposite the Cross Keys, three holes of different sizes – one for Daddy Bear, one for Mummy Bear, and one for Baby Bear. Marvellous! Though I couldn't help being glad that Baby Bear's – my – hole was at the other end of the seat from the birds' nest, where the wood was distinctly splodgy.

'Mucky little bastards,' Mrs Fenner observed affectionately. She brushed some segments of regurgitated bluebottle on to the earth floor before pulling down her bloomers and getting on with it.

We didn't talk much. There was no need. The sense of companionship was all. I felt quite sorry for poor constipated Mr Leach in his grey socks and polished shoes stuck there two doors away, all on his own.

The porthole in the door was too high up for me, seated, to see anything but the sky. I sat happy and mindless until Mrs Fenner said, at exactly the right moment, 'All good things have to come to an end. Pass us a bit o' paper, Sylvie, there's a good gal.'

Maud said it was time for my walk. I didn't know how this intelligence was revealed to her and did not dare to ask. Mrs Fenner, looking as if the very idea of a walk in St Awdry's was something novel, not to say barmy, demanded, 'Walk? What bloody for?'

'Sylvie needs the exercise. We can go round by the Swan, and up as far as the fields.'

'Oh ah.' Mrs Fenner received the suggestion without enthusiasm. 'Fields. What you want to go an' look at them fer?'

'Oh, ma!' exclaimed her daughter, who, after seven years in the city, had evidently acquired some of the townee's chronic sentimentality about the countryside. 'You know yourself it's nice up there.'

'Nice for cows.' But Mrs Fenner came along cheerfully enough.

Nobody in St Awdry's ever took a walk. In a world geared to the plough, the hoe, to cows to be brought in for milking, putting one foot in front of the other for pleasure was a daft idea if ever they heard one. There seemed to be hardly anybody but us alive in the village. At the side of one of the cottages which straggled along the unmetalled lane, a boy was looking for a bicycle puncture, moving the inner tube round in a basin of water, watching for bubbles. A black and tan dog, rolling on its back in the sandy roadway to get rid of its fleas, lifted its head to see who was coming along, sensed no threat, and went back to its rough and ready grooming. In a front garden a woman with a net over her hair and wearing a black cardigan in spite of the heat was cutting sweet williams.

'Arternoon!' Mrs Fenner greeted her politely, receiving in return what might or might not have been a nod.

'Stuck-up bit o' bacon!' remarked Mrs Fenner when we were past, but not sufficiently past not to be overhead. 'Acts like she's the Queen o' Sheba on account she used to work in the kitchen at Sandringham. Just because King Edward, bless him, once pinched it on the back stairs, don't mean we all got to bow down an' kiss her arse.'

The houses petered out and the fields began, boring, exactly as Mrs Fenner had intimated. There did seem to be an unnecessary amount of green in the world.

Mrs Fenner took out a handkerchief and wiped the sweat from her face. 'How long's this bloody walk goin' on?' she wanted to know.

Maud didn't answer. As ever, she knew what she was about. She led the way across the first field and a second, to a stile between hawthorn hedges where, after a quick survey of what lay beyond, she turned and waited for us to catch up. She was looking very pleased with herself.

'Get an eyeful o' that,' she commanded, when we arrived, hot and bothered. 'The same like always, year after year ever since I was Sylvie's age, *and* younger.'

The third field was less green than gold. Not the common gold of buttercups, but an orange shimmer, a gold that seemed to pulsate in the hot sun, that *was* the sun. The air was good enough to eat, heavy with the fragrance of apricots.

'Cowslips', Maud instructed me, as she helped me over the stile. 'Thought you might like to take a few back to your ma.'

A few! Surrounded by that sweet-scented treasure I ran about like one possessed. The stems yielded easily, a little juice exuding from the broken ends, enough to make my fingers sticky. I picked cowslips until I could hold no more, until I dropped as many as I picked, and still I went on picking.

Maud and her mother watched me unmoving, leaning on the stile side by side and apparently uninfected by my manic greed. Only when I ran to them and gave Maud my gatherings to hold, preliminary to beginning all over again, did she yank me back with a hand on the skirt of my dress.

'Leave some for somebody else, greedy guts!' She thrust the flowers under her mother's nose. 'Smell nice, don't they?'

I said, 'They smell of apricots.'

'Don't talk daft!' said Maud. Then, 'What do *you* say, ma?'

Mrs Fenner sniffed judiciously before pronouncing.

'Armpits? No. Tripe an' onions? No.' She buried her nose so deep in the flowers that golden pollen flecked her rosy cheeks. Then, with a radiant smile of recognition, 'Cowslips! Tha's what they smell like. Cowslips!'

How happy I was!

Mrs Fenner took a penknife and a piece of string out of her pocket, and sat down on the step of the stile. 'Gimme those.' Whilst I watched anxiously, afraid she was about to set all my effort at naught, she divided up the big bunch of cowslips into smaller bunches, cut some stems so short there was little left but the nodding flowerets, left others as I had picked them. She saw my eyes on her and sent me to an oak tree which grew in the hedge by the ditch, to see if I could find a nice little pincushion of moss, not too big, not too small, and no bloody bugs in it either.

I found the moss without difficulty. When I brought it back, she rammed the bright green pad into the heart of the cowslips; knotted the string, cut it, made a loop big enough to get your hand through in the piece that was left: felt for a hairpin in her hair to make a kind of anchorage at the other end. A lock of hair plopped down on her neck, which made us all laugh, and made me feel suddenly sure that my cowslips were going to be all right after all.

'Ma!' Maud exclaimed, her voice vibrant with love. 'You are a one!'

Mrs Fenner had made a cowslip ball, a small sun brought down on earth. She slipped the loop of string over my wrist. Its beauty was beyond words and I bore it back to Opposite the Cross Keys, myself made beautiful by the bearing of it.

When we were back in the scullery, Mrs Fenner made me dunk the ball in the bucket of water, just once, and then she hung it up to drain on a nail over the range, the excess water puddling the floor. Maud brought the kettle in from the living-room and filled it from the same bucket, taking no account of the ants and other small insects which were floating there. The difference between Maud's Salham St Awdry and her Norwich standards of hygiene enchanted me.

While she cut great doorsteps of bread and marge as against the paper-thin bread and butter for which my mother's tea table was justly famed, I slipped out of the back door and down to the privies. I didn't need to go, and if I had needed to, I would have held it in until I had company. I just wanted to see if Mr Leach's shoes and socks were still there.

They were; only just at that moment a woman came out of the Leaches' cottage and shouted 'Bert!' in a voice that shattered the sweet contentment of the place, the grasses, the nodding poppies. A moment later, a man of medium size, dressed in grey trousers, a white, long-sleeved shirt and a black, grey and red-striped tie that went well with the shoes and the socks with the fancy clox, came out of the Leach privy and hurried up the path. He was youngish, I thought – so far as, in my judgement, any grown-up was anything but bowed under the weight of years – even though the hair on the top of his head was thinning. His rounded shoulders, his nose advancing, chin retreating, gave him a sad and fretful look. He did not look as if he had accomplished much, down at the lav or anywhere else.

I wished I had the nerve to tell him about senna pods, which May Bowden swore by. Or that I were like Mrs Fenner who, I felt, would certainly have called out, in her rich, warm voice, 'Better luck next time, bor!' As it was, we both saw and pretended not to see each other.

Leaving Home

Laurie Lee

Laurie Lee

Leaving Home

From *As I Walked Out One Midsummer Morning*

This extract is from Laurie Lee's second autobiographical volume, in which he describes his departure from home in Stroud, his walk to London, and his months in Spain on the eve of the Spanish Civil War.

He starts out . . .

The stooping figure of my mother, waist-deep in the grass and caught there like a piece of sheep's wool, was the last I saw of my country home as I left it to discover the world. She stood old and bent at the top of the bank, silently watching me go, one gnarled red hand raised in farewell and blessing, not questioning why I went. At the bend of the road I looked back again and saw the gold light die behind her; then I turned the corner, passed the village school, and closed that part of my life for ever.

It was a bright Sunday morning in early June, the right time to be leaving home. My three sisters and a brother had already gone before me; two other brothers had yet to make up their minds. They were still sleeping that morning, but my mother had got up early and cooked me a heavy breakfast, had stood wordlessly while I ate it, her hand on my chair, and had then helped me pack up my few belongings. There had been no fuss, no appeals, no attempts at advice or persuasion, only a long and searching look. Then, with my bags on my back, I'd gone out into the early sunshine and climbed through the long wet grass to the road.

It was 1934. I was nineteen years old, still soft at the edges, but with a confident belief in good fortune. I carried a small rolled-up tent, a violin in a blanket, a change of clothes, a tin of treacle biscuits, and some cheese. I was excited, vain-glorious, knowing I had far to go; but not, as yet, how far. As I left home that morning and walked away from the sleeping village, it never occurred to me that others had done this before me.

I was propelled, of course, by the traditional forces that had sent many generations along this road – by the small tight valley closing in around one, stifling the breath with its mossy mouth, the cottage walls narrowing like the arms of an iron maiden, the local girls whispering, 'Marry, and settle down.' Months of restless unease, leading to this inevitable moment, had been spent wandering about the hills, mournfully whistling, and watching the high open fields stepping away eastwards under gigantic clouds . . .

And now I was on my journey, in a pair of thick boots and with a hazel stick in my hand. Naturally, I was going to London, which lay a hundred miles to the east; and it seemed equally obvious that I should go on foot. But first, as I'd never yet seen the sea, I thought I'd walk to the coast and find it. This would add another hundred miles to my journey, going by way of Southampton. But I had all the summer and all time to spend.

That first day alone – and now I was really alone at last – steadily declined in excitement and vigour. As I tramped through the dust towards the Wiltshire Downs a growing reluctance weighed me down. White elder-blossom and dog-roses hung in the hedges, blank as unwritten paper, and the hot empty road – there were few motor cars then – reflected Sunday's waste and indifference. High sulky summer sucked me towards it, and I offered no resistance at all. Through the solitary morning and afternoon I found myself longing for some opposition or rescue, for the sound of hurrying footsteps coming after me and family voices calling me back.

None came. I was free. I was affronted by freedom. The day's silence said, Go where you will. It's all yours. You asked for it. It's up to you now. You're on your own, and nobody's going to stop you. As I walked, I was taunted by echoes of home, by the tinkling sounds of the kitchen, shafts of sun from the windows falling across the familiar furniture, across the bedroom and the bed I had left.

When I judged it to be tea-time I sat on an old stone wall and opened my tin of treacle biscuits. As I ate them I could hear mother banging the kettle on the hob and my brothers rattling their tea-cups. The biscuits tasted sweetly of the honeyed squalor of home – still only a dozen miles away.

I might have turned back then if it hadn't been for my brothers, but I couldn't have borne the look on their faces. So I got off the wall and went on my way. The long evening shadows pointed to folded villages, homing cows, and after-church walkers. I tramped the edge of the road, watching my dusty feet, not stopping again for a couple of hours.

When darkness came, full of moths and beetles, I was too weary to put up the tent. So I lay myself down in the middle of a field and stared up at the brilliant stars. I was oppressed by the velvety emptiness of the world and the swathes of soft grass I lay on. Then the fumes of the night finally put me to sleep – my first night without a roof or bed.

Redmond O'Hanlon

Jungle Hysterics

From *Into the Heart of Borneo*

Redmond O'Hanlon, an academic and natural history book reviewer, and his friend James Fenton, a poet and journalist, decided to go into the jungles of Borneo. They knew very little about what to expect, and quickly found out from books that they'd need to find ways:

. . . of barring 1,700 different species of parasitic worm from your bloodstream and Wagler's pit viper from just about anywhere; of removing small, black, wild-boar ticks from your crotch with minimum discomfort (you do it with sellotape); of declining to wear a globulating necklace of leeches all day long; of sidestepping amoebic and bacillary dysentery, yellow and blackwater and dengue fever, malaria, cholera, typhoid, rabies, hepatitis, tuberculosis and the crocodile (thumbs in its eyes, if you have time, they say).

An SAS major gave them this advice:

'You'll find the high spot of your day,' said the major, 'is cleaning your teeth. The only bit of you you can keep clean. Don't shave in the jungle, because the slightest nick turns septic at once. And don't take more than one change of clothes, because you must keep your Bergen weight well down below sixty pounds. And don't expect your Iban trackers to carry it for you, either, because they have enough to do transporting their own food. So keep one set of dry kit in a sealed bag in your pack. Get into that each night after you've eaten. Powder yourself all over, too, with zinc talc – don't feel sissy about it – you'll halve the rashes and the rot and the skin fungus. Then sleep. Then get up at 5.30 and into your wet kit. It's uncomfortable at first, but don't weaken – ever; if you do, there'll be two sets of wet kit in no time, you'll lose sleep and lose strength and then there'll be a disaster. But take as many dry socks as you can. Stuff them into all the crannies in your pack. And, in the morning, soak the pairs you are going to wear in autan insect repellent, to keep the leeches out of your boots. Stick it on your arms and round your waist and neck and in your hair, too, while you're about it, but not on your forehead because the sweat carries it into your eyes and it stings. Cover yourself at night, too, against the mosquitoes. Take them seriously, because malaria is a terrible thing and it's easy to get, pills or no.

'Get some jungle boots, good thick trousers and strong shirts. You won't want to nancy about in shorts once the first leech has had a go at you, believe me. Acclimatise slowly. The tropics takes people in different ways. Fit young men here just collapse in Brunei. You'll think it's the end of the world. You can't breathe. You can't move. And then after two weeks you'll be used to it. And once in the jungle proper you'll never want to come out.

'It's a beautiful country and the Iban are a fine people. I was on the River Baram myself, but to go up the Rajang and the Baleh will be better for your purposes. That's a good plan. The Baleh is very seldom visited, if at all, up-river, and the Tiban mountains should be very wild indeed. They look small on a map, those mountains, but they're tough going. One steep hill after another. And you have to be good with a compass. Any questions? No. Good. Well done, lads, Goodbye and good luck.'

Fenton and O'Hanlon, stunned into silence, drove off and fell into a pub.

Some time later, O'Hanlon wrote:

It was time to go to bed. We washed our mess tins in the river, kicked out the fire on the beach, and stoked up the smoking-house fire with more wet logs. Slinging my soaking clothes from a tree with parachute cord, I rubbed myself down with a wet towel and, naked, opened my Bergen pack to pull out my set of dry kit for the night. Every nook and cranny in the bag was alive with inch-long ants. Deciding that anything so huge must be the Elephant Ant, and not the Fire ant, which packs a sting like a wasp, I brushed the first wave off my Y-fronts. Glancing up, I was astonished to see my wet clothes swarming with ants, too; a procession of dark ants poured down one side of the rope and up the other; and, all over my wet trousers, hundreds of different moths were feeding. I rummaged quickly in the outside Bergen pocket for my army torch. As my fingers closed on it, everyone else's little fingers seemed to close on my arm. I drew it out fast and switched on: Elephant Ants, this time with massive pincers, were suspended from hand to elbow. The soldiers had arrived. I flicked them off, gratified to hear yelps from James's basha as I did so. It was good to know they also went for poets.

Could things get worse? Read on!

The river twisted and turned and grew narrower, and the great creepers, tumbling down in profusion from two hundred feet above our heads, edged closer. The rapids and cascades became more frequent. We had to jump out into the river more often, sometimes to our waists, sometimes to our armpits, pushing the dugout up the shallows, guiding it into a side-channel away from the main crash of the water.

'*Saytu, dua, tiga – bata!*' sang Dana, which even we could reconstruct as one, two, three, and push.

The Iban gripped the round, algae-covered stones on the river-bottom easily with their muscled, calloused, spatulate toes. Our boots slipped into crevices, slithered away in the current, threatened to break off a leg at the ankle or at the knee. It was only really possible to push hard when the boat was still, stuck fast, and then Headmaster Dana would shout '*Badas!*' 'Well done!' But the most welcome cry became '*Npan! Npan!*': an invitation to get back in, quick.

Crossing one such deep pool, collapsed in the boat, the engine restarted, we found ourselves staring at a gigantic Bearded Pig sitting quietly on his haunches on the bank. Completely white, an old and lonely male, he looked at us with his piggy eyes. Dana, throwing his pole into the boat, snatched up his shotgun; Leon, abandoning the rudder, followed suit. Inghai shouted a warning, the canoe veered sideways into the current, the shotguns were discarded, the boat realigned, and the pig, no longer curious, ambled off into the jungle, his enormous testicles swaying along behind him.

We entered a wide reach of foaming water. The choppy river-waves, snatching this way and that, had ripped caves of soil out of the banks, leaving hundreds of yards of overhang on either side. There was an ominous noise of arguing currents ahead. The rapids-preamble – the white water, the moving whirlpools, the noise ahead – was longer and louder than it ought to have been.

With the canoe pitching feverishly, we rounded a sweeping bend; and the reason for the agitated river became obvious. The Green Heave ahead was much higher than any we had met. There was a waterfall to the left of the river-course, a huge surging over a ledge. The way to the right was blocked by thrown-up trees and piles of roots that had been dislodged upstream, torn out in floods, and tossed aside here against a line of rocks. There was, however, one small channel through; a shallow rapid, dangerously close to the main rush of water, but negotiable. It was separated from the torrent by three huge boulders.

Keeping well clear of the great whirlpool beneath the waterfall, Leon brought the boat to the base of this normal-size rapid. Dana, James and I made our way carefully up with the bow-rope.

Dana held the lead position on the rope; I stood behind him and James behind me. We pulled, Leon and Inghai pushed. The boat moved up and forward some fifteen feet and then stuck. Leon and Inghai walked up the rapid, and, hunching and shoving, rolled small rocks aside to clear a channel. We waited on the lip of the rock above, pulling on the rope to keep the long boat straight. At last Leon and Inghai were ready. But the channel they had had to make was a little closer to the waterfall. To pull straight we must move to our right. Dana pointed to our new positions.

It was only a stride or two. But the level of the river-bed suddenly dipped, long since scooped away by the pull of the main current. James lost his footing, and, trying to save himself, let go of the rope. I stepped across to catch him, the rope bound round my left wrist, snatching his left hand in my right. His legs thudded

into mine, tangled, and then swung free, into the
current, weightless, as if a part of him had been knocked
into outer space. His hat came off, hurtled past his
shoes, spun in an eddy, and disappeared over the lip of
the fall.

His fingers were very white; and slippery. He bites
his fingernails; and they could not dig into my palm. He
simply looked surprised; his head seemed a long way
from me. He was feeling underwater with his free arm,
impossibly trying to grip a boulder with his other hand,
to get a purchase on a smooth and slimy rock, a rock
polished smooth, for centuries, by perpetual tons of
rolling water.

His fingers bent straighter, slowly, edging out of
mine, for hour upon hour – or so it felt, but it must have
been seconds. His arm rigid, his fingertips squeezed out
of my fist. He turned in the current, spread-eagled. Still
turning, but much faster, he was sucked under; his right
ankle and shoe were bizarrely visible above the surface;
he was lifted slightly, a bundle of clothes, of no dis-
cernible shape, and then he was gone.

'Boat! Boat!' shouted Dana, dropping the rope,
bounding down the rocks of the rapid at the side,
crouched, using his arms like a baboon.

'Hold the boat! Hold the boat!' yelled Leon.

James's bald head, white and fragile as an owl's egg,
was sweeping round in the whirlpool below, spinning,
bobbing up and down in the foaming water, each orbit
of the current carrying him within inches of the black
rocks at its edge.

Leon jumped into the boat, clambered on to the
raised outboard-motor frame, squatted, and then, with
a long, yodelling cry, launched himself in a great
curving leap into the centre of the maelstrom. He
disappeared, surfaced, shook his head, spotted James,

dived again, and caught him. Inghai, too, was in the water, but he faltered, was overwhelmed, and swept downstream. Leon, holding on to James, made a circuit of the whirlpool until, reaching the exit current, he thrust out like a turtle and they followed Inghai down-river, edging, yard by yard, towards the bank.

Obeying Dana's every sign, I helped him coax the boat on to a strip of shingle beneath the dam of logs. James, when we walked down to him, was sitting on a boulder. Leon sat beside him, an arm round his shoulders.

'You be all right soon, my friend,' said Leon, 'you be all right soon-lah, my very best friend. Soon you be so happy.'

James, bedraggled, looking very sick, his white lips an open *O* in his black beard, was hyper-ventilating dangerously, taking great rhythmic draughts of oxygen, his body shaking.

'You be OK,' said Leon. 'I not let you die, my old friend.'

Just then little Inghai appeared, beaming with pride, holding aloft one very wet straw boater.

'I save hat!' said Inghai, 'Jams! Jams! I save hat!'

James looked up, smiled, and so stopped his terrible spasms of breathing.

He really was going to be all right.

Suddenly, it all seemed funny, hilariously funny. 'Inghai saved his hat!' We laughed and laughed, rolling about on the shingle. We giggled together until it hurt. 'Inghai saved his hat! Ingy-pingy saved his hat!' It was, I am ashamed to say, the first (and I hope it will be the last) fit of genuine medically-certifiable hysterics which I have ever had.

Leena Dhingra

Breaking Out of the Labels

From *Watchers and Seekers*

Leena Dhinga was born in India and spent the first few years of her life in Paris before coming to England. She describes the frustrations and pain of having had continually to cope with the 'label-fitting-fighting game' – resisting other people's kind and unkind attempts to define her according to their perceptions.

I first came to this country nearly thirty years ago during which time I have fallen into, fitted and resisted a series of multifarious labels from: a girl from India, an Indian girl, a coloured, a Paki, a black, a wog, an Asian, and recently graduated to becoming a member of an ethnic minority.

Recently when I was asked to give a talk as an Asian woman, I found myself reflecting more on what to say to fit the label than what to say to fit my own person. Recognising this deeply ingrained old pattern of label-fitting and label-fighting, I decided to embark on a retrospective survey into the meanings and effects of my labelled past.

When I first came to England it was in the mid-fifties. I was an eleven-year-old schoolgirl on my way to boarding school, and was, quite simply, a little girl from India. There was nothing to quarrel about there. Even the fact that I had not at the time arrived directly from India, but from Paris, where my family had found itself, having lost home and city to Pakistan following the partition, I was still a little girl from India. I knew that

India was free, and that we were refugees. From my father I knew both the Bengali and English versions of the poem by Tagore which had become the Indian national anthem and used to recite it to rhythm as I played hopscotch on the Paris pavements:

Thou art the/ruler/of the/minds/of all/people
Thou/dispenser/of India's/destiny
Thy/name/rises/in the/hearts/of the Punjab . . .

My mother always chose to remind me about being a refugee when she dispensed my pocket money: 'We are refugees . . . everything we have is by God's grace . . . we are lucky . . . must always share . . . and help others . . .' But I didn't really need any prompting by then, as it was always willingly that I would place the greater part of my money in the large Munich beer mug my father had been presented at some conference and which had since come to be known as my refugee mug.

London, though new, didn't feel strange at all. In fact it had a fairy-tale familiarity in my eleven-year-old eyes. I knew it from pictures I had seen, from stories I had heard and so many people appeared to have visited, passed through, studied or lived in it. And, of course, I knew it from the Monopoly board and the childhood magic that had been invested in the game through playing it with my cousins in the sunny Indian court-yards, sipping long lemon drinks and wrangling over the property cards. And I was pleased to find that even the train that was to take me away to my boarding school left from my favourite station, Kings Cross!

My cosmopolitan Quaker boarding school posed no threat to the three pillars of my identity: of being Indian, free and a refugee. And the three countries I flew in and out of so frequently, reinforced the meanings which I imbibed as Gandhi, dignity, and concern for others less fortunate than me. As an Indian girl in Paris, I came from the land of Gandhi. In India, I was part of a history and a caring present, and in boarding school, my tendency to the most enormous painful chilblains would invariably elicit tender concern from my housemother and reminders of my precious Indianness. It all fitted neatly and felt okay.

But the okayness of it all soon came to an end once I left the protected precincts of my boarding school and came to London. This time it was not to pass through as I usually did on my way to Paris for the holidays, but to stay, get a couple more 'O's, finish off my 'A's, prepare for an audition to Drama School and find a place to stay.

'Are you coloured?' said the voice on the phone.

'I beg your pardon?' was my reply.

'Where have you come from?' said the voice.

'From Paris,' said I.

'Are you French?' said the voice again.

'No, no no. I'm Indian,' came my reply.

'Sorry dear, but we can't take no coloureds here.'

Surprise ceded to shock, followed by indignation. A stink bomb had been thrown open and without realising it at the time I had absorbed its smell, as for my next call, I said:

'Excuse me, but, I am an Indian student calling about the room you advertised.'

Admittedly, I found accommodation, then and later, without much trouble and as the years went on I thought I was becoming quite blasé. When one of my theatre landladies said as I was leaving, 'I'm so sorry to see you go, you're such a lovely girl, even if you are Indian,' I corrected her as I kissed her goodbye saying, 'No, no, it is *because* I am Indian.' We both laughed, she with tears in her eyes. But the blaséness was only a thin shell, that covered, and protected me from the smell.

And so it was that I came to fall into the label-fitting-fighting game, and in the course of time became increasingly confused and bruised! For being 'coloured' was a muddly business, making less and less sense the more I learned. I learned, for instance, that there was a gradation of 'coloured', that it was more acceptable and more polite to be 'less' coloured. Paradoxically, however, this lessness was not necessarily correlated to pigmentation but to something more subtle, like packaging and presentation and the sincere persuasion that you were striving to be less . . . than you were.

But it was a losing battle anyway – and in spite of my beautifully enunciated drama school diction, I remained 'so awfully nice and really such a pity that nearly, but not quite, right'. And to add to my dismay I learned that remarks like, 'If you cut your hair darling you could easily pass off for Italian, Greek or Spanish, and no one need ever know . . .' were said with the best of intentions and meant to be taken as a compliment.

India! Free! Refugee! Gandhi, Dignity and Concern! The three certain pillars of my identity started to become marks of vulnerability as additional meanings got grafted on through new tripartite experiences.

On my longed-for visits to India I was the girl who'd gone away, always a guest, a visitor from Paris or London, staying in other people's houses, fitting in with their ways. Around me Gandhi was energetically being woven into the web of mythical meanings and symbols, being concretised into statues and stamped as a new road name just as energetically as his message was being forgotten. The poverty which wrenched my heart felt too unjust and belied all sense of dignity. And being a refugee, which I had understood as being concerned for others – now also assumed a new meaning: that of being uprooted of having no home and no refuge of my own.

In Paris, outside my parents' circle of India = Gandhi and philosophy, I encountered *'l'Inde mystèrieuse'* – occasionally mysterious to the point of nonexistence. Buying stamps in one of the outlying Paris districts in 1960, I was handed back my letter and told: 'Simply India won't do! You must put which India: French India? British India? Portuguese India? . . .'

In England, Richard Attenborough hadn't made his film and Gandhi had not yet been elevated to being more than a half-naked fakir. And India? Well . . . it had been part of the Empire, hadn't it? Was there anything else to know?

Nothing fitted neatly any more and everything felt far from okay. I flew between here and there trying to find the where, or the way, to make it fit again. In the meantime, I learned chameleon-like to change colours to suit circumstances.

'A Tiger is a tiger', my father used to say, to remind me of a particular story among the hundreds that had enchanted my childhood. In it, an orphaned tiger cub is adopted by a herd of goats. He learns their ways, how to chew grass, and 'bleat', both of which he manages with some difficulty. One day a big tiger from the jungle appears and the herd runs away – except for the little tiger who stays and continues to 'graze'. The jungle tiger stops in his tracks, whereupon the little tiger 'bleats' him a greeting. On hearing this big tiger roars in amazement and amusement. The story ends with the big tiger taking the little one to a still pond to show him the similarities in their reflections; introducing him to meat – whereupon the little one discovers his real teeth – and finally inviting him into the depths of the jungle where he rightfully belongs and can discover the mystery of his own true self.

In travelling around and searching – for my tiger or jungle – I managed to escape the Paki onslaught and by the time I came back as a 'returning resident' I was part of the throng of 'invading Asians'! During my absence, however, more than the labels had changed and feeling like Rip Van Winkle awakening from the long night, I discovered that a whole new generation had come into being. More vocal and less timid than me, they had even assumed a label of their own, that of the Black identity.

It was like discovering a fellowship of little tigers like me, seeing reflections in each other and sharing a whole new world of common experience and history. I was initiated and introduced to new ideas – about colonialism, imperialism, eurocentricism – perspectives which healed and eased. The scarred and bruised pillars re-emerged: Gandhi; dignity; and a concern for others: a shared reality.

And now, suddenly to ethnic minority! Ethnic minority? Which one fits me? Which one encompasses my reality? And then next year what will the label be? Enough! I'm stopping. Setting myself free. No more label-fitting or fighting for me. Neither am I searching for tigers or jungles any more – just beginning to roar . . .

Spiritual
Survival

Grace Nichols

Grace Nichols

Spiritual Survival

An essay from *Let It Be Told*

Let It Be Told is a collection of essays by black women in Britain, discussing their experiences and their outlook on life as revealed in their writing. Grace Nichols was born in Guyana in 1950 and is a short-story writer, journalist, novelist and poet. She came to Britain in 1977, and this is her response to being asked about herself as a black woman and a writer.

Sacred Flame

Our women
the ones I left behind
always know the taste
of their own strength –
bitter at times it might
be

But I
armed only with my mother's smile
must be forever gathering
my life together like scattered beads.

What was your secret mother –
the one that made you a woman
and not just Akosua's wife

With your thighs you gave
a generation of beautiful children
With your mind you willed the crops
commanding a good harvest

With your hands and heart
plantain soup and love

But the sacred flame of your woman's
kra you gave to no man, mother
Perhaps that was the secret then –
the one that made you a woman
and not just Akosua's wife.

(i is a long memoried woman)

As a writer I feel strongly multi-cultural and very Caribbean. If I have to describe myself as coming from a particular part of the world, I like to think of myself as coming from the Caribbean. Most of my work is created out of that culture which embraces so much. The Caribbean has one of the richest, most fascinating cultures you can hope to find anywhere; though this may sound like a cliché, for me it's true. OK, it has its poverty and backwardness, but just thinking about all the different cross-influences and mixtures – Amerindian, African, Asian, European – gets me high.

I keep being amazed at how much of Africa still remains in the Caribbean, when you consider the disruption caused by slavery and the whole European colonising experience. You have the presence and influence of the indigenous people in the region too. I feel a kinship with the Amerindian people of Guyana, for example, their myths and legends. I've used some of their legends in my children's stories. The Guyana hinterland is very much in my psyche so that part of me feels a bit South American and the incredible destruction of the Aztec/Inca civilisation also informs our heritage.

. . . up past the Inca ruins
and back again
drifting onto Mexican plains
the crumbling of golden gods
and Aztec rites
speak for themselves . . .

(Of Golden Gods)

Then of course you have the influences of the different immigrant groups who came out to the Caribbean: East Indians, Chinese, and Portuguese. So my voice as a writer has its source in that region. I feel a concern for the Caribbean and its economic and political future.

Wake up Lord
brush de sunflakes from yuh eye

Back de sky and while Lord
an hear dis mudda-woman cry
on behalf of her presshah down people

God de Mudda/God de Fadda/God de Sista
God de Brudda/God de Holy Fire . . .

As a writer and poet I'm excited by language, of course. I care about language, and maybe that's another reason why I write and continue to write. It's the battle with language that I love. When it comes to writing poetry, it is the challenge of trying to create or chisel out a new language that I like. I like working in both standard English and creole. I tend to want to fuse the two tongues because I come from a background where the two worlds, creole and standard English, were constantly interacting, though creole was regarded, obviously, as the inferior by the colonial powers when I was growing up and still has a social stigma attached to it in the Caribbean.

I think this is one of the main reasons why so many Caribbean poets, including myself, are now reclaiming our language heritage and exploring it. It's an act of spiritual survival on our part, the need (whether conscious or unconscious) to preserve something that's important to us. It's a language that our foremothers and forefathers struggled to create and we're saying that it's a valid, vibrant language. We're no longer going to treat it with contempt or allow it to be misplaced.

I don't think the only reason I use creole in my poetry is to preserve it, however. I find using it genuinely exciting. Some creole expressions are so vivid and concise, and have no equivalent in English. And there comes a time when, after reading a lot of English poetry, no matter how fine (I love the work of quite a few English poets), I want something different; something that sounds and looks different to the eye on the page and to the ear. Difference, diversity and unpredictability make me tick.

I have a natural fear of anything that tries to close in on me, whether it's an ideology or it's a group of people who feel that we should all think alike because we're all women or because we're all black, and there's no room to accommodate anyone with a different view.

I can't subscribe to the 'victim-mentality' either, which seems to like wallowing in 'Look what they've done to us'. It's true that black women have carried much more than their share of hardships along the way. But I reject the stereotype of the 'long-suffering black woman' who is so strong that she can carry whatever is heaped upon her. There is a danger of reducing the black woman's condition to that of 'sufferer', whether at the hands of white society or at the hands of black men. I know too many black women with a surmounting spirit and with their own particular quirkiness and sense of humour to know that this isn't true.

In the early days when I first started reading my poetry I was taken to task by a few women who wanted to know why I didn't write about or focus on 'the realities' of black women in Britain: racial discrimination, bad housing, unemployment, etc., and this poem came as a kind of response to that:

Of course when they ask for poems about the 'Realities' of black women

what they really want
at times
is a specimen
whose heart is in the dust

a mother-of-sufferer
trampled/oppressed
they want a little black blood
undressed
and validation
for the abused stereotype
already in their heads

           or else they want
           a perfect song

I say I can write
no poem big enough
to hold the essence

           of a black woman
           or a white woman
           or a green woman

and there are black women
and black women

             like a contrasting sky

of rainbow spectrum

touch a black woman
you mistake for a rock
and feel her melting
down to fudge

cradle a soft black woman
and burn fingers as you trace
revolution
beneath her woolly hair

and yes we cut bush
to clear paths
for our children
and yes we throw sprat
to catch whale
and yes
if need be we'll trade

a piece-a-pussy
than see the pickney dem
in the grip-a-hungry-belly

still there ain't no
easy belly category

                for a black woman
                or a white woman
                or a green woman

and there are black women
strong and eloquent
and focussed

and there are black women
who always manage to end up
frail victim

and there are black women
considered so dangerous
in South Africa
they prison them away

      maybe this poem is to say

that I like to see
we black women
full-of-we-selves walking

      crushing out
      with each dancing step

the twisted self-negating
history
we've inherited

      crushing out
      with each dancing step

I'm also very interested in mythology. It has created certain images and archetypes that have come down to us over the ages, and I have observed how destructive, however inadvertently, many of them have been to the black psyche. As children we grew up with the all-powerful male white God and the biblical associations of white with light and goodness, black with darkness and evil. We feasted on that whole world of Greek myths, European fairy-tales and legends, princes and princesses, Snowhites and Rapunzels. I'm interested in the psychological effects of this on black people even up to today, and how it functions in the minds of white people themselves.

Once when I was taking part in a discussion on this subject, a white woman in the audience made the point that darkness was frightening. Children were afraid of the dark because they couldn't see in the dark. I agreed with her. I myself put on lights if I'm feeling a bit uneasy for some reason. But what the white imagination has done is to transfer this terror of darkness to a whole race. I'm fascinated, to say the least, how whenever a white person – whether writer, painter or dramatist – has to portray an evil, ugly or a monstrous character they inevitably make that character black. It's as if the white imagination can't help depicting this because that's the image that comes to mind in relation to evil or terror.

I think that white people have to be aware of this in their psyche and question it if they don't want to be trapped in this clichéd vision.

I feel we also have to come up with new myths and other images that please us.

Although *The Fat Black Woman's Poems* came out of a sheer sense of fun, of having a fat black woman doing exactly as she pleases, at the same time she brings into being a new image – one that questions the acceptance of the 'thin' European model as the ideal figure of beauty. The Fat Black Woman is a universal type of figure, slipping from one situation to the other, taking a satirical, tongue-in-cheek look at the world:

> Shopping in London winter
> is a real drag for the fat black woman
> going from store to store
> in search of accommodating clothes
> and de weather so cold
>
> Look at de frozen thin mannequins
> fixing her with grin

and de pretty face salesgals
exchanging slimming glances
thinking she don't notice

*(The Fat Black Woman
Goes Shopping)*

Literature isn't a static thing. The myths of old were
created by the poets of old and remain powerful sources
of imagination, to be drawn on again and again.
Odysseus in his rolling ship did a lot for mine as a child
and I am grateful. But we have to keep on creating and
reshaping. We have to offer our children something
more than gazing at *Superman 1, Superman 2, Superman 3*
and possibly *Superman 4*, so that when they look out on
the world they can also see brown and black necks
arching towards the sun. So that they could see themselves represented in the miraculous, and come to sing
their being.

In *i is a long memoried woman*, the woman is something
of a mythic figure. She breaks the slave stereotype of the
dumb victim of circumstance. She is a woman of complex
moods who articulates her situation with vision. Her
spirit goes off wandering, meeting women from other
cultures. She's a priestess figure and employs sorcery
when necessary.

I require an omen, a signal
I kyan not work this craft
on my own strength
alligator teeth
and feathers
old root and powders
I kyan not work this craft
this magic black

on my own strength
Dahomney lurking in my shadows
Yoruba lurking in my shadows
Ashanti lurking in my shadows
I am confused
I lust for guidance.

(Omen)

At this point I must say that it isn't easy writing about myself as a writer and the piece very nearly 'not got done'. Immediately after I was asked by Lauretta, I began to suffer from what is conveniently known as 'writers' block', even though I was at first very enthusiastic about the idea. The truth is, I don't like answering too many questions about my work and how I work. Half of the time I really don't know the answers. In any case I believe that my feelings on a range of issues come out much better in my poems and writings. Poetry, thankfully, is a radical synthesising force. The erotic isn't separated from the political or spiritual, and a lot gets said.

It's difficult to answer the question. 'Why I write' because writing isn't a logical activity. It's a compulsion like a disease that keeps you alive. At a simple conscious level I would say that I write because writing is my way of participating in the world and in the struggle for keeping the human spirit alive, including my own. It's a way of sharing a vision that is hopefully life-giving in the final analysis.

In writing, I feel that I have some control over the world, however erroneous this might be. I don't have to accept things as they are, but can recreate the world a little more to my own liking. I don't have to accept a world that says that the black woman is invisible, for example, or a world that tries to deny not only black women but women on the whole, the right to participate in the decision-making necessary for change and an improved quality of life. I can introduce my own values. I can write against stereotypes as I've done with *The Fat Black Woman's Poems*.

Questions such as 'How do you see yourself? Do you see yourself as Black first or as a Woman first?' sometimes asked by other women freeze up the brain and become irritating because it seems like arbitrary cross-examination. It isn't something you even sit down and think about – 'Now am I black first or am I woman first?' These make up one's essential being, whatever that might be. 'Am I a committed writer?' I think I am committed to my own truth. 'Which is more important to me, the women's struggle or the fight against neo-colonialism and political repression?' I can't compartmentalise myself. I hate all forms of oppression. South Africa makes me feel chronically ill inside. I can't shut it out. And if a woman is being oppressed, say by her man at home, then that personal immediate oppression is just as hateful as the one by the state.

'Do I write as a "woman" or simply as a "writer"?' I don't really know but I believe that my perceptions cannot help but be influenced by my sex, race, cultural background and a heap of other factors, like the kind of childhood I had. Life is a mystery to me too. I myself am still working towards clarification. Maybe if I had all the answers I wouldn't be writing at all.

Study Material and Activities

Christy Brown: 'The Letter 'A''

Christy Brown's book was first published in 1954. In 1987 *Under the Eye of the Clock* was published – written by Christopher Nolan, similarly disabled, it is his story told through the character of Joseph Meehan. Both books convey a sense of anguish at how deeply buried a keen mind could be inside a disabled body. Both show how powerfully their mothers believed in them.

> But nobody wounded like him could deserve a chance at life. Better dead said the crones, better dead said history, better jump in at the deep end decided her strong soul as she heard his crestfallen cry. His mother it was who treated him as normal, tumbled to his intelligence, tumbled to his eye-signalled talk, tumbled to the hollyberries, green yet, but holding promise of burning in red given time, given home.
>
> *Christopher Nolan*

Compare this, above, with Christy Brown's mother – 'She had nothing in the world to go by . . . she just knew . . . out of love.'

Christopher Nolan/Joseph describes his frustrations like this:

> He saw how others saw him but he wanted to show everyone how truly wrong they were. Fenced in on all sides he heard things he was never meant to hear and

he saw things he was never meant to see. How could he ever get his chance to let folk see what they never thought existed?

How do I conquer my body, mused the paralysed boy. Paralysed I am labelled, but can a paralytic move? My body rarely stops moving. My arms wage constant battle trying to make me look a fool. My smile which can be most natural, can at times freeze, thereby making me seem sad and uninterested. Two great legs I may have, but put my bodyweight on them and they collapse under me like a house of cards. How then can I convey to folk that the strength in my legs can be as normal as that of the strongest man?

The sketches below are taken from *Annie's Coming Out.* Like Christy Brown and Christopher Nolan, Annie McDonald has cerebral palsy, and her body was bent badly.

The nurses in the hospital thought they could only feed her as shown in Diagram 2; the position was so difficult for her that her tongue-thrusts, part of her disablement, often made her reject her food. If the nurses gave up too quickly, she was often left hungry. Her normal intelligence, desperately buried inside, was

Diagram 1

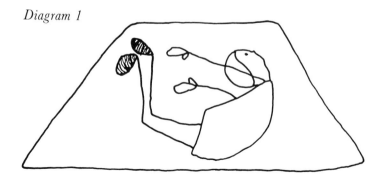

Diagram 2

discovered by a hospital psychiatric worker, Rosemary Crossley, and the book is their joint account of how Annie was encouraged to communicate and reveal her real self.

All three writers, Christy Brown, Christopher Nolan, and Annie McDonald, describe the real joy and relief of being able to 'speak' to the world through their books. Still frustrations and sadness remain at the limitations nonetheless that writing sets:

Speech has always been one of the biggest obstacles in my endeavour to make ordinary contact with people. It has been the one aspect of my handicap that has caused me the bitterest pain, for without speech one is practically lost, curtained off from other people, left wishing to say a million things and not able to say one. Writing is all very well, but there are some emotions that cannot be conveyed, that cannot be 'felt' through the written word alone. Writing may be immortal, but it does not bridge the gap between two human beings as the voice may, and oh, I would rather have an hour's fierce argument with a pal or a few moments of soft chatter with a girl than write the greatest book on earth.

Christy Brown

1 What changes in thinking are necessary to break down prejudice and ignorance about disablement?

2 Do you have any experience of this as a disabled person or as a friend of a disabled person?

3 What adjustments has your school made or does your school need to make to give proper and rich opportunities to disabled students?

Buchi Emecheta: 'What They Told Me'

4 Big Mother is a powerful presence in this extract. What do we know about her? Write down all the things that the young Buchi Emecheta liked and loved about her – she had 'all the patience in the world', for example.

Valente Malangatana's poem about birth (opposite) is written to her mother, but see what she says about her grandmother.

To the Anxious Mother

Into your arms I came
when you bore me, very anxious
you, who were so alarmed
at that monstrous moment
fearing that God might take me.

Everyone watched in silence
to see if the birth was going well.
Everyone washed their hands
to be able to receive the one who came from Heaven
and all the women were still and afraid.
But when I emerged
from the place where you sheltered me so long,
at once I drew my first breath
at once you cried out with joy.
The first kiss was my grandmother's.
And she took me at once to the place
where they kept me hidden away.
Everyone was forbidden to enter my room
because everyone smelt bad
and I all fresh, fresh
breathed gently, wrapped in my napkin
But grandmother, who seemed like a madwoman,
always looking and looking again
because the flies came at me
and the mosquitoes harried me
God who also watched over me
was my old granny's friend.

Valente Malangatana

5 Adults other than parents can be very important in a
child's life. Has there ever been anyone like this for
whom you felt a great deal of love?

Big Mother's name, Nwakwaluzo, means 'this child cleared the path'. Buchi Emecheta tells us about girl children 'clearing the path' for the coming of male children . . . 'It was almost like a command: she must have a male baby brother.' What does she say about the importance of the male in Ibo culture?

Male children have been important in many cultures through history.

> *To please, to be useful to us, to make us love and esteem them, to educate us when young, to take care of us when grown-up; to advise, to console us, to render our lives easy and agreeable. These are the duties of women at all times, and what they should be taught in their infancy.*
>
> *Rousseau, an 18th-century philosopher*

When boys are encouraged to think of themselves as stronger and more significant, are there dangers in store for their adult relationships?

Some societies now regard such attitudes to girls and women as sexist, and have made huge leaps to 'clear the path' for all children to grow up into a world of equal worth and opportunities. Some societies still regard girls and women as living within the protection of their males.

6 What are your thoughts and experiences?

Beryl Bainbridge: 'Funny Noises with Our Mouths'

7 Beryl Bainbridge conjures up several different memories to create 'a sense of family life'. She remembers characters, conversations, sayings, and habits, and she weaves them together in this short piece to give a sense of the

whole. Can you do the same with the people you live with? Think of the kinds of conversations they have, including the things they say over and over again; their relationships with each other as you perceive them. One or two incidents might serve to illustrate your points.

There is a sense of distance over time about 'Funny Noises with Our Mouths'. Beryl Bainbridge is looking back over a number of years, almost as if it were another world as well as another time.

There's something of this 'feel' about 'The Picnic in Jammu':

The Picnic in Jammu

Uncle Ayub swung me round and round
till the horizon became a rail
banked high upon the Himalayas.
The trees signalled me past. I whistled,
shut my eyes through tunnels of the air.
The family laughed, watching me puff
out my muscles, healthily aggressive.

*This was late summer, before the snows
come to Kashmir, this was picnic time.*

Then, uncoupling me from the sky, he
plunged me into the river, himself
a bough with me dangling at its end.
I went purple as a plum. He reared
back and lowered the branch of his arm
to grandma who swallowed me with a kiss.
Laughter peeled away my goosepimples.

*This was late summer, before the snows
come to Kashmir, this was picnic time.*

After we'd eaten, he aimed grapes at
my mouth. I flung at him the shells of
pomegranates and ran off. He tracked
me down the river-bank. We battled,
melon-rind and apple-core our arms.
'You two!' grandma cried. 'Stop fighting, you'll
tire yourselves to death!' We didn't listen.

This was late summer, before the snows
come to Kashmir and end children's games.

Zulfikar Ghose

Both Beryl Bainbridge and Zulfikar Ghose have this
sense of family life – experienced as children a long time
ago.

What is it about the poem that gives us this sense of
time vanished?

Eva Hoffman remembers this moment from her childhood in Poland before her Jewish family went to live in
Canada:

I am walking home from school slowly, playing a
game in which it's forbidden to step on the cracks
between the slabstone squares of the pavement. The
sun is playing its game of lines and shadows. Nothing
happens. There is nothing but this moment, in which
I am walking toward home, walking in time. But
suddenly, time pierces me with its sadness. This
moment will not last. With every step I take, a sliver
of time vanishes. Soon, I'll be home, and then this,
this nowness will be the past, I think, and time seems
to escape behind me, like an invisible current being
sucked into an invisible vortex. How can this be, that
this fullness, this me on the street, this moment which
is perfectly abundant, will be gone? It's like that time

I broke a large porcelain doll and no matter how much I wished it back to wholeness, it lay there on the floor in pieces. I can't do anything about this backward tug either. How many moments do I have in life? I hear my own breathing: with every breath, I am closer to death. I slow down my steps: I'm not home yet, but soon I will be, now I am that much closer, but not yet . . . not yet . . . not yet . . . Remember this, I command myself, as if that way I could make some of it stay. When you're grown up, you'll remember this. And you'll remember how you told yourself to remember.

Lost in Translation (Heinemann)

8 Do you have a single and distant memory? Perhaps it's something that has stayed in your mind. Maybe talking at home with others might jog your memory, or a photograph might spark it off.

Clifford Dyment: 'My Father, the Carpenter'

Reread the description of Will Dyment's parting from his family as he set off for war. Start from the lines, 'It was early still, still smelling of night' and go on to the end of the chapter.

Now read this extract. It comes from *Eleni* by Nicholas Gage (Fontana). It is the writer's description of when he saw his mother for the last time. It was 1948, and she was one of the many victims of the civil war that tore Greece apart after World War II had already taken its toll.

It was the look in her eyes as she put the chain around my neck that filled me with the awful knowledge of what she was doing. She was giving me this charm, which felt so heavy on my chest, as a consolation for losing her. I didn't want the silver cross, I wanted the warmth of her body, the comfort of her face, which was now so white that it seemed I could see through to the bones which pulled the skin taut. She had made me promise to be brave, and I resolved to keep that vow, to be as stalwart as the Spartan boy while the fox gnawed at his bowels, so that she would come back to me.

Kanta was crying, but I stood silent, frowning in the sunlight, as my mother set off down into the ravine, the last woman in line. Every few steps she would turn around as if to reassure herself that we were still there.

Standing on the edge of the great chasm, we watched the dark line of women descend into the depths until they were hidden by the green foliage along the stream flowing through the bottom of the ravine. After about five minutes the serpentine line reappeared on the other side, crawling like a column of ants up to the base of the hill of the Prophet. If I hadn't known that she was last in line, I never could have recognised her as the small brown-and-black figure that stopped every now and then to look back.

The line of women continued on into the distance, around the base of the hill. There was a spot where the path curved around a myrtle tree and out of sight. I concentrated all my energy on holding my mother in my sight. When she reached the spot where she would disappear from view, she stopped and turned around again. As she looked toward the cliff where she knew we were watching, she raised her hand above her head.

Years later I would have moments, even days, when my mother's features would blur and grow dim in my memory's eye, but I never lost the clear image of her gesture and the way she looked on that green and gold summer day when she turned around to wave to me for the last time.

Will Dyment and Eleni Gatzoyiannis left their families behind in different circumstances and in different wars, but what do these two partings share?

9 Is there a parting in your life that remains vivid to you? There are also the partings that are caused not by death but by people moving away. Sometimes they move away to another place, and sometimes they move emotionally away and this can be just as hard to bear. If you have parted from someone important to you, does your story have a sad or a happy ending?

Nicholas Gage dedicated his book in the following way:

To the memory of

Eleni Gatzoyiannis
Alexandra Gatzoyiannis • Vasili Nikou
Spiro Michopoulos • Andreas Michopoulos

He also chose to quote at the start of his book the last words of the famous novel by the American writer Thornton Wilder (1897–1975) as an unusual kind of epigraph to his terrifying story of how a mother fought to save her children in a war. Thornton Wilder's novel describes the effects of the disastrous breaking of the 'finest bridge in all Peru' in July 1714. The book ends with the following elegy for the power of love:

But soon we shall die and all memory of those five will have left the earth, and we ourselves shall be loved for a while and forgotten. But the love will have been enough; all those impulses of love return to the love that made them. Even memory is not necessary for love. There is a land of the living and a land of the dead and the bridge is love, the only survival, the only meaning.

10 What single words and phrases contribute most powerfully to the skilful and tender picture that Clifford Dyment conveys of his father as a carpenter?

11 Is there a member of your family whom you could describe in poetry or prose like this? Someone you love, and who enjoys doing something that, like Will Dyment's carpentry, brings his or her character to life?

Paul Bailey: 'The Professor'

Both the extracts tell us that Paul Bailey's parents loved him, and that he remembers them with love.

'Long Distance' by Tony Harrison is also about love:

Long Distance

Though my mother was already two years dead.
Dad kept her slippers warming by the gas,
put hot water bottles her side of the bed
and still went to renew her transport pass.

You couldn't just drop in. You had to phone.
He'd put you off an hour to give him time
to clear away her things and look alone
as though his still raw love were such a crime.

He couldn't risk my blight of disbelief
though sure that very soon he'd hear her key
scrape in the rusted lock and end his grief.
He *knew* she'd just popped out to get the tea.

I believe life ends with death, and that is all.
You haven't both gone shopping; just the same,
in my new black leather phone book there's your
    name
and the disconnected number I still call.

What do Dad's actions tell us?
What is the last verse about and why is it so powerful?

Paul Bailey and Tony Harrison look back as adults at
their parents. They have found that both the company
of elderly parents and the force of their memories move
them.

The relationship between parents and their children
is always strong. It often isn't easy, sometimes it isn't
loving, but it always matters, and the loss of a parent or
a child is always deeply traumatic. Where and how does
this powerful relationship start?

12 Look at the tensions in Paul Bailey's two extracts: his
father wants him to read and brings home Charles
Dickens's *Nicholas Nickleby*. Paul doesn't read it for years
– until he's 15. It's another 28 years before the full force
of the gift strikes him. His mother doesn't understand
his need to act nor why he takes such 'funny' parts. Yet
she turns up, and although her remarks are tart, she's
proud. Between the writer and his parents is a huge
gap: two worlds collide. Can you explain the tensions
and how it is that they still love each other?

13 What tensions exist in your own family or with the
people you live with?

14 What might you especially remember with respect and love about members of your family if you were parted from them? Do you already have reason to miss them?

15 Is there anyone who remembers what it was like when you were born?

J B Priestley: 'Three Delights'

In groups discuss:

a) Do you share Priestley's love of football?

b) Do you have your own version of the 'long trousers' which you really enjoy wearing?

c) How do you feel about 'not going'? Have you ever 'not gone' when you desperately wanted to?

16 What delights are there in your own life – spending time with close friends? Reading? Collecting something? Listening to music?

Choose three of your 'delights' to write about.

William Cooper: 'Scenes . . .'

It might be hard for us to imagine a time when the traffic was sparse, slow-moving and horse-drawn, but this was a feature of William Cooper's childhood that he remembers quite clearly. Seventy years on he also recalls the marbles and the cigarette cards with all their original thrills. He seems comfortable and happy with these memories – unlike V S Pritchett, another famous writer, who begins *his* autobiography with unease:

This is the year of my seventieth birthday, a fact that bewilders me. I find it hard to believe. I understand now the look of affront I often saw in my father's face after this age and that I see in the faces of my contemporaries. We are affronted because, whatever we may feel, time has turned us into curiosities in some secondhand shop.

He goes on . . .

I have before me two photographs. One is, I regret, instantly recognisable: a bald man, sitting before a pastry board propped on a table, and writing. He does little else besides sit and write. His fattish face is supported by a valence of chins; the head is held together by glasses that slip down a bridgeless nose that spreads its nostrils over a moustache. He is trying to find some connection with the figure in another picture taken fifty years ago. He knows that the young fellow sitting on the table of a photographers in Paris, a thin youth of twenty with thick fairish hair, exclaiming eyebrows, loosely grinning mouth and the eyes raised to the ceiling with a look of passing schoolboy saintliness, is himself. The young one is shy, careless, very pleased with himself, putting on some impromptu act; the older one is perplexed. The two, if they could meet in the flesh, would be stupefied and the older one would certainly be embarrassed.

17 Can you find a photograph of yourself as a young child, say around five or six years old? You might be in school uniform, or be part of a family group. Look at it carefully and see if you can recognise yourself in that small person – or is it hard to believe that that was you?

What were you like then? What sort of things did you do? Who did you love, and who did you spend time with?

Compare it with a recent photograph or a good hard look in the mirror. How have you changed, and in how many ways?

Write about those two people.

Roald Dahl: 'The Great Mouse Plot'

This is Roald Dahl's preface to his book:

> An autobiography is a book a person writes about his own life and it is usually full of all sorts of boring details.
>
> This is not an autobiography. I would never write a history of myself. On the other hand, throughout my young days at school and just afterwards a number of things happened to me that I have never forgotten.
>
> None of these things is important, but each of them made such a tremendous impression on me that I have never been able to get them out of my mind. Each of them, even after a lapse of fifty and sometimes sixty years, has remained seared on my memory.
>
> I didn't have to search for any of them. All I had to do was skim them off the top of my consciousness and write them down.
>
> Some are funny. Some are painful. Some are unpleasant. I suppose that is why I have always remembered them so vividly. All are true.

18 Choose one of your own funny, painful or unpleasant childhood memories to write about.

Look again at Roald Dahl's definition of an autobiography.

Here are some other comments on autobiographical
writing.

Margaret Walker wrote:

> About my autobiography . . . I'm not writing a
> confession. I don't have to tell anything I don't want
> to tell.

When Maya Angelou was asked, 'Do you consider
your quartet to be autobiographical novels or autobiographies?', she replied:

> They are autobiographies. When I wrote *I Know Why
> the Caged Bird Sings*, I wasn't thinking so much about
> my own life or identity. I was thinking about a
> particular time in which I lived and the influences of
> that time on a number of people. I kept thinking,
> what about that time? What were the people around
> young Maya doing? I used the central figure – myself
> – as a focus to show how one person can make it
> through those times.

Toni Cade Bambara recalls:

> I used to assign my students a writing/thinking
> exercise: remember how you used to get all hot in the
> face, slide down in your seat, suddenly have to tie
> your shoe even though you were wearing loafers back
> then in the fourth grade whenever Africa was
> mentioned or slavery was mentioned? Remember the
> first time the mention of Africa, of Black, made your
> neck long and your spine straight, made the muscles
> of your face go just so? Well, make a list of all the
> crucial, relevant things that happened to you that
> moved you from hot face to tall spine; then compose a

short story, script, letter, essay, poem that make that experience of change available to the young brothers and sisters on your block.

Toni Cade Bambara also says, 'We all do (*write autobiographically*) . . . That is, whomsoever we may conjure up or remember or imagine to get a story down, we're telling our own tale . . .'

(The three pieces by Margaret Walker, Maya Angelou and Toni Cade Bambara are taken from *Black Women Writers at Work*, Oldcastle Books.)

19 What good reasons for writing autobiography have you come across in other people's writing?

20 What do you see as good reasons for writing your own autobiographical accounts?

Sylvia Haymon: 'A Day with the Fenners'

Sylvia Haymon's visit to the Fenners' took her into a different world. Country people in the early 1900s were very poor. She could afford to be fascinated because she was returning to a life of relative comfort in Norwich, but to the Fenners her adventure was for them a daily reality of harsh poverty. There is a study of East Anglian life called *Akenfield: Portrait of an English Village* by Ronald Blythe. It is an account by, for example, forge workers, farm workers, wheelwrights, district nurses – all the people who lived and worked there in the first part of this century. Their memories gave Blythe the material for his book. It is largely the world of the Fenners and you will be able to see and feel some more of their world in these extracts.

a)

It was very hard living indeed for the family. There were seven children at home and father's wages had been reduced to 10s. a week. Our cottage was nearly empty – except for people. There was a scrubbed brick floor and just one rug made of scraps of old clothes pegged into a sack. The cottage had a living-room, a larder and two bedrooms. Six of us boys and girls slept in one bedroom and our parents and the baby slept in the other. There was no newspaper and nothing to read except the Bible. All the village houses were like this.

Our food was apples, potatoes, swedes and bread, and we drank our tea without milk or sugar. Skim milk could be bought from the farm but it was thought a luxury. Nobody could get enough to eat no matter how they tried. Two of my brothers were out to work. One was eight years old and he got 3s. a week, the other got about 7s. Our biggest trouble was water. There was no water near, it all had to be fetched from the foot of a hill nearly a mile away 'Drink all you can at school', we were told – there was a tap at school. You would see the boys and girls filling themselves up like camels before they left school so that they would have enough water to last the day.

Leonard Thompson, farm worker aged 71

b)

People believed in religion then, which I think was a good thing because if they hadn't got religion there would have been a revolution. Nobody would have stuck it. Religion disciplined us and gave us the strength to put up with things. The parson was very respected. He could do what he liked with us when he felt like it. One day he came to our house and told my eldest sister, who was eleven, to leave school. 'I think you needn't finish,' he said. 'You can go and be maid to old Mrs Barney Wickes, now she has lost her husband.' Mrs Barney Wickes was blind and my sister was paid a penny a day out of Parish Relief to look after her.

Leonard Thompson

c)

There was no main water. We all drank from the ponds or the pump or from some wells. It was nothing for me to nurse where the boiled water was bright green! As for my equipment, well I will tell you. I had a saucepan for boiling up my instruments, a spirit stove and several enamel bowls. I carried all this stuff about from house to house in a huge American cloth bag which I made myself. I used to have to strain all the village water through muslin before I dared use it. As well as these things, I carried plenty of odd pieces of mackintosh and a big bundle of clean rags – torn sheets from the better-off houses mostly. We never had nearly enough dressings. As for drugs, well there was aspirin and little else. People in great pain might be given occasional morphia by the doctor. Nothing much. On the whole, people took pain and illness for granted; they weren't very frightened. They didn't worry very much. They supposed they would get better. Nor did they seem fearful of death. They had all worked so hard and so long, I suppose there was a kind of comfort in it.

Marjorie Jope, district nurse aged 79

21 In groups, discuss which aspects of the lives described in *Opposite the Cross Keys* and *Akenfield* shock or move

you most when you compare them with your life now.

22 Interview some older people you know, friends or people in your family. Take notes or use a tape recorder, and ask them to describe features of their childhoods. Then write up their stories as vividly and accurately as you can.

Laurie Lee: 'Leaving Home'

Laurie Lee's mother lets him go, blessing him. She doesn't question what he wants to do – at least, not out loud. When he looks back, he sees 'the gold light die behind her'.

23 What might this suggest to us about her and about his relationship with her? Look through the rest of the extract to find evidence of the tension he was feeling between looking back and thinking about home and walking on 'to discover the world'. Arrange your notes in two columns, and you'll be able to see if he feels more strongly in one direction or another.

24 Could you do the same thing for your own life, if you were to imagine setting off now? Where would the tensions lie for you?

Where was Laurie Lee going?
The first part of his journey ends with London:

Cleo, my girlfriend, was somewhere out there; hoarding my letters (I hoped) and waiting. Also mystery, promise, chance, and fortune – all I had come to this city to find. I hurried towards it, impatient . . .

Months later came the realisation that 'I could go anywhere I liked in the world.' This seems to have loosened his ties, for a while, with his old romantic self. Having already parted with Cleo, he looks for another kind of relationship, which he finds with a girl called Nell. He is heady with freedom, and disregards her plea: 'Take me with you. I wouldn't be any trouble.'

I felt light-headed, detached, and heartless. 'Take me with you' was something I was also hearing from other girls, who seemed not to have noticed me till now. For the first time I was learning how much easier it was to leave than to stay behind and love.

Cleo hadn't been his first love; elsewhere he describes Ellie, sixteen and a server in a cake shop. He has brought his inseparable friend Arnold to see her:

Large, beautiful, with Spanish hair and eyes, skin tight with flesh as an apple, Ellie slipped from the stile and faced us boldly, smiling a slow, fat smile. I watched her closely as her eyes moved over us, heavy-lidded as a sleepy owl.

Her lazy gaze finally rested on Arnold. It was an excruciating moment of doubt. 'Push off, you,' she murmured. Arnold didn't argue; he gave a thin dry cough and went.

I was alone with the girl in a smell of warm rain, feeling handsome, jaunty, and chosen. Ellie stood thigh-deep in the glittering grass like a half-submerged tropic idol.

'Lift us up on that wall, come on,' she said. 'I'm dead scared of things in the grass.'

Cuddles in the grass put even Arnold out of mind:

> 'Look what I got,' she said, fishing behind the wall. She produced a bag full of crusty doughnuts. 'We won't need no supper. I get 'em from work. I live on 'em practically.' She gave me one and sank her teeth into another. 'You're a boy all right,' she said. 'You got a nerve.' She took another deep bite, and her teeth came out red with jam.
>
> I couldn't forget Ellie after that, and there were vivid dreams at night, when her great brown body and crusty roundness became half girl and half groceries. My sleep knew the touch of gritty sugar on the lips and the crisp skin fresh from the bakery, enclosing who knew what stores of sweet dough, of what light dabs of jam hidden deep . . .

Compare this with H E Bates writing about his first love, Con, after he had plucked up courage to write to her:

> But there was a reply; we were to meet. We met, as I remember it, in the First Class waiting-room on Number Three platform at Kettering station. There is no practical reason whatever for there ever being erected a plaque on a house in London saying *H E Bates lived here;* but if there were any justice whatever in the history of railways and twentieth-century novelists there should be a plaque on the door of the First Class waiting-room on Platform Number Three at Kettering station, saying *H E Bates loved here.*
>
> Con appeared to me even more hauntingly beautiful, on that second meeting, than at the first.

The Vanished World (Michael Joseph)

137

Much later:

> One warm fine spring evening we wandered along the
> wooded banks of a brook, probably a small tributary
> of the River Welland. Primroses, kingcups, white and
> purple violets and Shakespeare's Lady-smocks
> bloomed everywhere about the marshy earth. After
> some time I stopped to climb a stile and then,
> suddenly turning my head to look for Con, found
> myself caught up in an unexpected, swift and
> passionate embrace, and then kissed long, fully and
> ardently on the lips.
>
> How I recovered from this totally unexpected but
> delicious ravaging of my boyhood innocence I find it
> hard to say; it sometimes seems to me not at all
> impossible that I might have been left speechless for
> the rest of my life. There was certainly, at that
> ecstatic moment, nothing to say; nor could I have
> said it if I had wanted to; instead I could only offer
> my lips in further sacrifice, surrendering to an ardour
> returned by lips ecstatic, compulsive and not wholly
> inexperienced. It was no longer a question of sweet,
> devoted friendship; the moment was more like the
> fusion of two white-hot wires. I was more than slightly
> shocked and intoxicated in consequence; it was now a
> case, in Herrick's words again, of:
>
>> *'Thou Art my Life, my Love, my Heart,*
>> *The Very Eyes of me;*
>> *And last command of every part*
>> *To live and die for thee.'*

25 Does anything in life – books you read, lessons in
school, talks with friends, love for family – prepare you
for the love you feel for a first partner?

Why do you think first loves often end sadly, or with

a sense of disappointment, or just seem funny after-wards?

What was it like when you first felt this kind of love, or what would you like it to be like?

Redmond O'Hanlon: 'Jungle Hysterics'

26 a) What aspects of survival in the Borneo jungle would challenge you most? Is there anything, for example in the SAS major's warnings and advice, that might put you off going altogether?

b) 'It was time to go to bed.' What does this phrase conjure up for you when you think of an ordinary bedtime at home? Could you cope with a swarming procession of ants?

For some people the urge to travel is very strong.
Rabbi Lionel Blue writes:

The excitement of travel hit me when I was very young. Whenever anything nasty made the headlines – Mosley, Hitler or unemployment – I opted out of my surroundings and daydreamed of far-off places like Southend or Margate. I stood silently in the children's playground, enraptured by place names, reciting silently the list of London stations like a litany.

Blue Horizons (Coronet)

Some just have an urge to get away from home and go anywhere. Here is Bill Bryson writing about his home in Iowa, USA:

I come from Des Moines. Somebody had to . . . By Iowa standards, Des Moines is a Mecca of cosmopolitanism, a dynamic hub of wealth and education, where people wear three-piece suits and dark socks, often simultaneously. During the annual state high school basketball tournament, when the hayseeds from out in the state would flood into the city for a week, we used to accost them downtown and snidely offer to show them how to ride an escalator or negotiate a revolving door. This wasn't always so far from reality. My friend Stan, when he was about sixteen, had to go and stay with his cousin in some remote, dusty hamlet called Dog Water or Dunceville or some such improbable spot – the kind of place where if a dog gets run over by a truck everybody goes out to have a look at it. By the second week, delirious with boredom, Stan insisted that he and his cousin drive the fifty miles into the county town, Hooterville, and find something to do. They went bowling at an alley with warped lanes and chipped balls and afterwards had a chocolate soda and looked at a *Playboy* in a drugstore, and on the way home the cousin sighed with immense satisfaction and said, 'Gee thanks, Stan. That was the best time I ever had in my whole life!' It's true.

I had to drive to Minneapolis once, and I went on a back road just to see the country. But there was nothing to see. It's just flat and hot, and full of corn and soybeans and hogs. I remember one long, shimmering stretch where I could see a couple of miles down the highway and there was a brown dot beside the road. As I got closer I saw it was a man sitting on a box by his front yard in some six-house town with a name like Spiggot or Urinal, watching my approach with inordinate interest. He watched me zip past and in the rear-view mirror I could see him still watching me going on down the road until at last I disappeared into a heat haze. The whole thing must have taken about five minutes. I wouldn't be surprised if even now he thinks of me from time to time.

Granta: *The Best of Travel* (Penguin)

27 a) Have you had any travelling adventures?
   b) Would you like to get away from where you are living at the moment? (What would family and friends say?)
   c) If you could go anywhere in the world, where would you go, and why? Write about one or more of these.

Leena Dhingra: 'Breaking out of the Labels'

Leena Dhingra's essay shows that there is a close re-lationship between labelling and name-calling. Someone who says 'Indian' and then says, 'You're such a lovely girl, even if you are Indian' is unconsciously close to the person who freely uses 'Paki' as a deliberate insult. In both cases racism is at work.

28 Read Leena Dhingra's essay again and chart the labels she has had to resist so far in her life. Sort them into two categories; those intended to be neutral and those meant to hurt. Then discuss the impact of both.

Some words are singled out by people who want to be most offensively racist. Leena Dhingra refers to 'Paki' which carries similar weight to 'nigger'.

It is a short step from 'Paki' and 'nigger' to a devastating denial of humanity. Huck in *Huckleberry Finn* spins a story to his Aunt Sally to explain his late arrival, and he says:

'It wasn't the ground – that didn't keep us back but a little. We blowed out a cylinder-head.'

'Good gracious! Anybody hurt?'

'No'm. Killed a nigger.'

'Well, it's lucky; because sometimes people do get hurt.'

If this isn't a 'body', a person who is killed, then there's no death to report. Valerie Bloom writes this:

Yuh Hear Bout?

Yuh hear bout di people dem arres
Fi bun dung di Asian people dem house?
Yuh hear about di policeman dem lock up
Fi beat up di black bwoy widout a cause?
Yuh hear bout di MP dem sack because
   im refuse fi help
im coloured constituents in a dem fight
   'gainst deportation?
Yuj noh hear bout dem?
Me neida.

Lenna Dhingra ends her essay with a powerful sense of self. She is setting herself free of labels, 'just beginning to roar.'

Audre Lorde, who describes herself as a 'black lesbian feminist warrior poet', said in interview that she would like to share with the younger generation of black women writers and writers in general these attitudes:

Not to be afraid of difference. To be real, tough, loving. And to recognise each other. I can tell them not to be afraid to feel and not to be afraid to write about it. Even if you are afraid, do it anyway because we learn to work when we are tired, so we can learn to work when we are afraid. Silence never brought us anything. Survive and teach; that's what we've got to do and to do it with joy.

Maud Sulter also resists labelling and celebrates difference. She has her own self-definition:

Africa	Pale Mother	Roots
	I am I	
	See me	
	Perceive me	
	But I	
	Shall name	
	My self.	

29 Use any of the thoughts above and anything from your own experience to write about 'breaking free of labels'.

Grace Nichols: An Essay

Grace Nichols gives many reasons for writing, and one is an excitement with language. She likes writing in standard English and in creole, and has a strong sense of reclaiming a language heritage . . . 'a language that our foremothers and forefathers struggled to create and we're saying that it's a valid, vibrant language.'

Valerie Bloom, who comes from Jamaica, also writes about the importance of language:

It is clear that language is closely associated with identity. There has been a well-documented struggle in Jamaica (and other Caribbean islands) to give status to the first language of the people . . .

Edward Kamau Braithwaite coined the term 'Nation Language' to give dignity and status to the way we talk . . .

Most Jamaicans refer to their first language as 'Patois' . . .

Dialect poetry (to describe poetry written in patois) is a standard term.

Valerie Bloom writes a lot of dialect poetry.

Compare 'Mek Ah Ketch Har' with 'Let Me Get Hold of Her'; here are a couple of verses:

Mek Ah Ketch Har

Onoo hole mi yaw, onoo hole mi good,
No mek mi get weh do,
For ah mus kill har if mi ketch har,
Dat mawga gal name Sue.

Onoo no tell mi fe shet mo mout,
Ah mus sleep a jail tenite!
Long time now she dah fool roun mi,
An teday ah gwine bus a fight.

Let Me Get Hold of Her

Just hold on to me, hold me tight,
Don't let me get away, will you?
Because I'll kill her if I get hold of her,
That skinny girl called Sue.

Don't tell me to shut my mouth,
I'm sure to sleep in jail tonight!
For too long now she's been messing me
    around,
And today I'm going to have to fight.

Alice Walker adds on to the notion of language heritage the intensely personal routes it travels on:

> Yet so many of the stories that I write, that we all write, are our mothers' stories. Only recently did I fully realize this: that through years of listening to my mother's stories of her life, I have absorbed not only the stories themselves, but something of the manner in which she spoke, something of the urgency that involves the knowledge that her stories – like her life – must be recorded . . . . She had handed down respect for possibilities – and the will to grasp them . . . . Guided by my heritage of love and beauty and a respect for strength – in search of my mother's garden, I found my own.

30 Are you conscious of having a heritage? – of inheriting a language, a culture, part of an understanding of yourself through the things your family have passed onto you? If so, does this make you feel good about yourself or is it something you're trying to break free from?

31 As well as having an inheritance, Grace Nichols also feels fiercely herself. 'I have a natural fear of anything that tries to close in on me,' she writes, 'whether it's a group of people who feel that we should all think alike because we're all black, and there's no room to accommodate anyone with a different view.' In the last paragraph of her essay she says life is still a mystery to her – she's still looking for it to be clearer. Do you think it helps to be part of a group? To feel things are partly worked out for you because you're female, male, black, Asian, white, young?

32 Grace Nichols' poem 'Holding My Beads' tells us what she feels. What could you write?

Holding My Beads

Unforgiving as the course of justice
Inerasable as my scars and fate
I am here
a woman . . . with all my lives
strung out like beads
                  before me

It isn't privilege or pity
that I seek
It isn't reverence or safety
quick happiness or purity
             but
the power to be what I am/   a woman
charting my own futures/   a woman
holding my beads in my hand

Note to the Teacher

The extracts in this collection are arranged in seven broad, but by no means exclusive, themes:

Birth
Christy Brown: *The Letter 'A'*
Buchi Emecheta: *How They Told Me*

Family Memories
Beryl Bainbridge: *Funny Noises with Our Mouths*
Clifford Dyment: *My Father, the Carpenter*
Paul Bailey: *'The Professor'*

Childhood
J B Priestley: *Three Delights*
William Cooper: *Scenes . . .*

Childhood Adventures
Roald Dahl: *The Great Mouse Plot*
Sylvia Haymon: *A Day with the Fenners*

Leaving Home
Laurie Lee: *Leaving Home*

Adult Adventures
Redmond O'Hanlon: *Into the Heart of Borneo*

Awareness of Race
Leena Dhingra: *Breaking Out of the Labels*
Grace Nichols: *Spiritual Survival*

Wider Reading

ABSE, DANNIE, *A Poet in the Family* (Hutchinson)

ANGELOU, MAYA, *I Know Why the Caged Bird Sings* (Virago)

BATES, HE, *The Vanished World* (Michael Joseph)

BEWICK, THOMAS, *My Life* (The Folio Society)

BLISHEN, EDWARD, *Sorry, Dad* (Hamish Hamilton)

BLIXEN, KAREN, *Out of Africa* (Penguin)

CHAPLIN, SID, *The Smell of Sunday Dinner* (Frank Grantham)

CONRAD, JOSEPH, *The Mirror of the Sea* (Methuen)

DAVIES, W H, *The Autobiography of a Super Tramp* (Oxford)

GRAVES, ROBERT, *Goodbye to All That* (Penguin)

KITCHEN, FRED, *Brother to the Ox* (Penguin)

LEIGH FERMOR, PATRICK, *Three Letters from the Andes* (John Murray)

LAYE, CAMERA, *The African Child* (Collins)

LEE, LAURIE, *A Moment of War* (Viking)

LEVI, PRIMO, *If This Is a Man* (Penguin)

LLEWELYN DAVIES, MARGARET (ED.), *Life as We Have Known It* (Virago)

MARKHAM, BERYL, *West with the Night* (Virago)

MWDAWAR, JEAN, *A Very Decided Preference* (Oxford)

NAIPAUL, V S, *The Middle Passage* (André Deutsch)

PLATH, SYLVIA, *Letters Home* (Faber)

RATUSHINSKAYA, IRINA, *In the Beginning* (Sceptre)

SHEPARD, ERNEST, *Drawn from Memory* (Penguin)

WASHINGTON, BOOKER T, *Up from Slavery* (Airmont Publishing Company, New York)

Acknowledgements

We are grateful to the following for permission to reproduce material:

Authors' Agents for extracts 'Nicholas Nickelby' and 'The Duchess of Marlborough' from *An Immaculate Mistake* by Paul Bailey; Bogle-L'Overture Publishers Ltd for extracts from an essay and poem 'Mek Ah Ketch Har' ('Let Me Get Hold of Her'), *News from Babylon* by Valerie Bloom; Constable & Co Ltd for extracts from *Opposite the Cross Keys* by Sylvia Haymon; Authors' Agents for extracts from *Boy* by Roald Dahl, (Jonathan Cape Ltd/Penguin Books); Andre Deutsch Ltd for extracts from *As I Walked Out One Midsummer Morning* & *I Can't Stay Long* both by Laurie Lee; J. M. Dent & Sons Ltd for an extract from *The Railway Game* by Clifford Dyment; the Author, Leena Dhingra for her short story 'Breaking out of Labels' from *Watchers and Seekers* (The Women's Press 1987); Faber & Faber Ltd for extracts from *My Left Foot* by Christy Brown; Authors' Agents for poem 'Picnic in Jammu' by Zulfikar Ghose; Granta Publications Ltd for an extract from Beryl Bainbridge *Autobiography* No 14, Winter 1984; Authors' Agents for poem 'Long Distance' by Tony Harrison from *Tony Harrison Selected Poems* (Penguin 1987); Karnak House for poem 'Holding my Beads' by Grace Nichols from *The Fat Black Woman's Poems* (Virago 1984); Macmillan London for extracts from *From Early Life* by William Cooper; Dr. Theo Vincent on behalf of the Author for poem 'To the Anxious Mother' by Valente Malangatana; Authors' Agents for an extract by Grace Nichols from *Let it be Told* by Laurette Ngcobo; OGWUGWU AFO for an extract from *Head Above Water* by Buchi Emecheta; Authors' Agents for extracts from *Into the Heart of Borneo* by Redmond O'Hanlon (Hamish Hamilton/Penguin Books); Authors' Agents for extracts from *Delight* by J. B. Priestley (Heinemann).

We are grateful to the following for permission to reproduce photographs:

Camera Press, London, for Roald Dahl (photo: Nick Powell); Fanny Dubes for Grace Nichols; Laurie Lee for his photo of himself as a young man; Penguin Books Australia Ltd for illustrations from *Annie's Coming Out* by Rosemary Crossley and Anne McDonald; Popperfoto for Christy Brown.

LONGMAN GROUP UK LIMITED
*Longman House, Burnt Mill, Harlow, Essex CM20 2JE, England
and Associated Companies throughout the World.*

© Longman Group UK Limited 1992

First published 1992
ISBN 0 582 08837 2

*Set in 11/13 point Baskerville, Linotron 202
Produced by Longman Malaysia Sdn Berhad
Printed in Malaysia by PA*